THE IVY LEAGUE ROCK AND ROLL QUIZ BOOK

by Jack Lechner

A Delilah Book

Distributed by the Putnam Publishing Group New York

Copyright © 1983 by Jack Lechner

A DELILAH BOOK
Delilah Communications Ltd.
118 E. 25 Street
New York, New York 10010

ISBN: 0-933328-62-1
Library of Congress Catalog Card Number: 82-74039

Manufactured in the U.S.A.
First printing 1983

All rights reserved. No part of this book may be reproduced or transmitted in any form or by any means, electronic or mechanical, including photocopying, recording or by any information storage and retrieval system, without permission in writing from the Publisher.

Special Thanks to
Vikki DiDonato and Kathryn Greene

BOOK DESIGN: VIRGINIA RUBEL

ACKNOWLEDGMENTS

I'd like to thank the people who served as advisors and guinea pigs while this book took shape:

Sam Bayer, John Pomeranz, Reuben Radding, Jim Hewitt, Terrilee Edwards, Dean Inouye, Brian Risby, Dora Edelson, Paul Cain, Andrew Cain, Ira and Susan Lechner, and a guy who was reading *Circus* magazine outside the Hecht Co., in Tysons Corners, VA. Also to the last guinea pig, Lisa Cortes.

Thanks to the employees of the NTI Tysons 4 Cinema, where much of this was written between shows; and to the Washington Metro, for a smooth ride.

A tip of the hat to Jeannie and Missy at Delilah; and thanks to the Washingtonian magazine, for keeping me off the streets.

And most of all, love to Judi, who got me sane and happy enough to write it.

JACK LECHNER
New Haven, CT
November 22, 1982

CONTENTS

QUESTIONS

Same Name	12
Identity Crisis	13
Can We Call You Bruce?	14
Santa Without A Clause	15
Mr. Moonlight	16
Stormy Weather	18
Will The Real Baldemar Huerta Please Stand Up?	19
Hello, It's Me	20
I Write The Songs	22
You Can All Join In	23
Mass Production	24
All By Myself	26
Hot Spaces	27
She's A Woman	28
Meaningless But True	28
I Got A Woman	29
Under The Covers	30
Man In The Glass Booth	33
One Pill Makes You Larger...	34
Taking Care of Business	36
Words Of Love	37
Get It Right The First Time	37

We Gotta Get Out Of This Place	38
Body Language	39
Get Together	40
Leader Of The Pack	42
Pack Of The Leader	42
My Little Town	43
London Calling	44
With A Little Help From My Friends	46
A Night At The Opera	47
Two For The Show	47
Freeze Frame	48
Celluloid Heroes	50
Sleeping With The Television On	51
It's Alive	52
Rocker Mortis	52
Selling Out	53
You're Entitled	54
I Call Your Name	54
On The Road	56
I Love Rock And Roll	56
Off The Record	57
One Hit Wonders	58
I Fought The Law	59
Combat Rock	61
Rockin' All Over The World	61
Point Of Order	62
Where I'm Coming From	63
Between The Lines	64
Who Wrote The Book Of Love	66
Different Drum	68
No Bassist In Fact	69
ROCK LOCKS	**70**
Juke Box Heroes	77
Cry Of Love	78
Love That Dirty Water	79
Dancing In The Street	81
Speaking Words Of Wisdom	82
He's So Fine	84
Feel Like A Number	84
Girls Talk	86
The Ivy League Rock Quiz	87
ANSWERS	**88**

THE IVY LEAGUE ROCK AND ROLL QUIZ BOOK

INTRODUCTION

Q: **What does rock and roll have to do with the Ivy League?**

A: That's like asking what Hall has to do with Oates. Ivy Leaguers aren't just bearded coughdrop brothers who listen to Mozart all day. Yale, Harvard, and Columbia have produced their share of rockers—and if you don't believe me, try the last quiz in this book. And more students and professors are discovering the magic in the music and the music in themselves all the time.

Q: **But what does this book have to do with the Ivy League?**

A: Well, not only is the Ivy League where I go to school (Yale 1984, boola boola), but it's where I learned about rock. When I unpacked my stack of classical and jazz albums freshman year, my roommates knew just

INTRODUCTION

what to do—two months after they first played me *Who's Next* and *Led Zeppelin IV*, I was playing acoustic guitar and reading *Rolling Stone*. Two months after that, I was playing electric guitar and reading *Creem* and *Circus*. Before I knew it, I was hopelessly in love with the music and had written this—*thing*.

Q: *The Ivy League Rock Quiz Book?*

A: Yeah, carefully designed to tease you, please you, amuse you, and confuse you. If you have any suggestions or questions, please send them to me in care of :
Delilah Books, 118 East 25 Street, NY, NY, 10010.

Q: **Who put the bomp in the bomp-bomp-a-lomp?**

A: You can find out for yourself—just turn the page.

QUESTIONS

THE IVY LEAGUE ROCK AND ROLL QUIZ BOOK

SAME NAME

In the 1960's, the Irish group *Them* had a hit with "Here Comes The Night." In the 1970's, the *Beach Boys* had a hit with "Here Comes The Night." Not a cover, the second song was an entirely different tune (<u>disco</u>, yet!) sharing only its title with Van Morrison's raspy sounding *Them* song. Song titles cannot be copyrighted. Here are some other performers or groups who shared a title, but not a song. What are the titles?

1. Led Zeppelin, Neil Sedaka
2. Kenny Rogers, Little River Band, Styx
3. Earth, Wind, & Fire; The Manhattans
4. Donna Summer, Dion
5. Don McLean, Carole King
6. Fabian, Loverboy
7. The Animals, The Electric Light Orchestra
8. David Bowie, Irene Cara
9. The Crazy World of Arthur Brown, The Pointer Sisters
10. Tom Petty and the Heartbreakers, Barbra Streisand
11. John Lennon, Pink Floyd
12. Roy Orbison, The Motels
13. Them, U2, Laura Branigan

See page 90 for answers.

THE IVY LEAGUE ROCK AND ROLL QUIZ BOOK
IDENTITY CRISIS

Each of these songs was written about or inspired by a famous musician or actor. Who?

1. "Killing Me Softly With His Song," Roberta Flack
2. "Hey Hey, My My (Into the Black)," Neil Young
3. "Suite: Judy Blue Eyes," Crosby, Stills, Nash
4. "Dancing With Mr. D.," The Rolling Stones
5. "She Said She Said," The Beatles
6. "You're So Vain," Carly Simon
7. "Candle In The Wind," Elton John
8. "Oh! Carol," Neil Sedaka
9. "Sister Morphine," The Rolling Stones
10. "Willie," Joni Mitchell
11. "Our House," Crosby, Stills, Nash, & Young
12. "Diamonds and Rust," Joan Baez
13. "Delta Lady," Joe Cocker
14. "Puppy Love," Paul Anka
15. "How Do You Sleep?" John Lennon

On a different tack, identify the artists who performed each of these tributes to the late John Lennon:

16. "Here Today"
17. "Life Is Real"
18. "Empty Garden"
19. "All Those Years Ago"

See page 91 for answers.

13

THE IVY LEAGUE ROCK AND ROLL QUIZ BOOK

CAN WE CALL YOU BRUCE?

Who is the performer that bears this nickname?

1. The Boss
2. The King
3. The Ox
4. Captain Trips
5. The Fish
6. The Godfather of Soul
7. The Killer
8. The Lizard King
9. Runt
10. The Big Man
11. Slowhand
12. The Captain (as in Tennille)
13. The Fat Man
14. Blood
15. Herman
16. The Thin White Duke
17. Bonzo
18. The Walrus of Love

AND:

19. The Glimmer Twins
20. The Nurk Twins

See page 92 for answers.

THE IVY LEAGUE ROCK AND ROLL QUIZ BOOK

SANTA WITHOUT A CLAUSE

Name changes are as common for rock groups as for rock stars. Match the discarded name with the group that discarded it.

1. Carl and the Passions
2. Soft White Underbelly
3. The Hourglass
4. The Golliwogs
5. Johnny and the Moondogs
6. Levon and the Hawks
7. The New Yardbirds
8. The High Numbers
9. The Primettes
10. Little Boy Blue and the Blue Boys
11. The Beefeaters
12. The Big Thing
13. Tom and Jerry
14. The Deltas
15. The Warlocks

A. The Grateful Dead
B. Simon and Garfunkel
C. The Supremes
D. Chicago
E. The Who
F. The Band
G. Blue Oyster Cult
H. The Allman Brothers Band
I. Led Zeppelin
J. Creedence Clearwater Revival
K. The Beach Boys
L. The Byrds
M. The Rolling Stones
N. The Beatles
O. The Hollies

EXTRA CREDIT: *Identify the British group that was so bad once upon a time that its name changed after every gig!*

See page 93 for answers.

THE IVY LEAGUE ROCK AND ROLL QUIZ BOOK
MR. MOONLIGHT

These pairs of bands each shared one member. Who was that member?

1. Cream; Derek & The Dominoes
2. The James Gang, The Eagles
3. The Modern Lovers; The Talking Heads
4. The Small Faces; The Who
5. Traffic; Blind Faith
6. The Sex Pistols; Public Image Ltd
7. Spooky Tooth; Foreigner
8. The Byrds; Crosby, Stills, Nash, & Young
9. Free; Bad Company
10. The Guess Who; Bachman-Turner Overdrive
11. The Faces; The Rolling Stones
12. The Grateful Dead; Kingfish
13. The Zombies; Argent
14. Quicksilver Messenger Service, Jefferson Starship
15. The Moody Blues; Wings
16. Emerson, Lake, & Palmer; Asia
17. Mountain; West, Bruce, & Laing
18. The Animals; War
19. Southside Johnny & the Asbury Jukes; The E Street Band
20. The Nice; Emerson, Lake, & Palmer (not #16)

See page 94 for answers.

MYSTERY ROCK STAR #1

This sweetly smiling choirboy grew up to be nobody's angel!

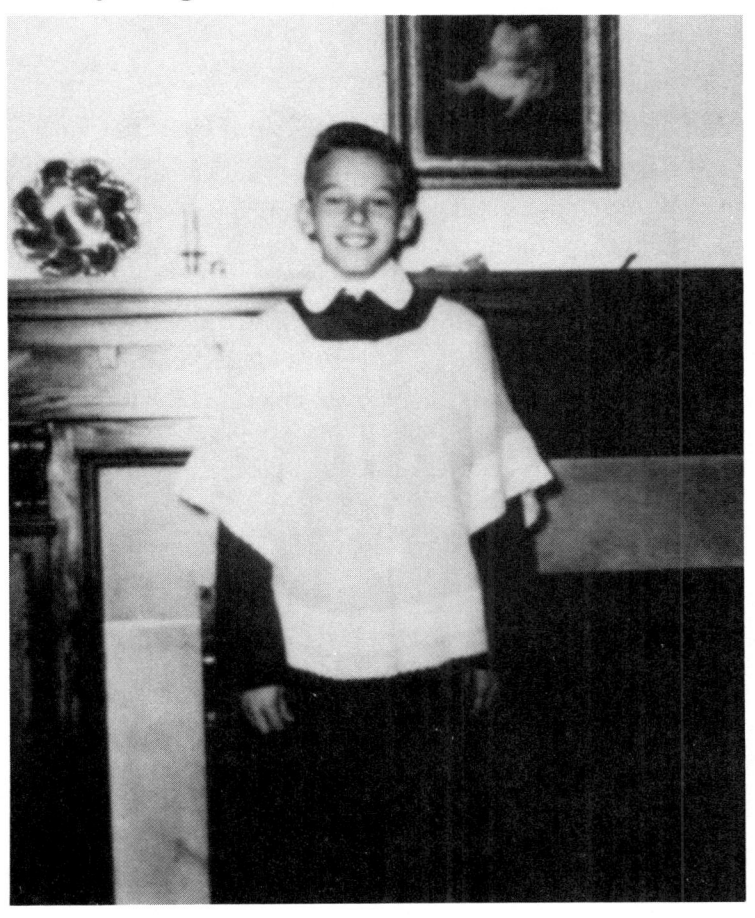

See page 142 for answers.

THE IVY LEAGUE ROCK AND ROLL QUIZ BOOK
STORMY WEATHER

Fill in the weather word missing from the song title.

1. "Have You Ever Seen the_____," Creedence Clearwater Revival
2. "And the_____ Cried Mary," Jimi Hendrix
3. "Like A _____," Neil Young
4. "Summer_____," Seals and Crofts
5. "Riders on the_____," The Doors
6. "_____Strikes," Lou Christie
7. "Don't Eat the Yellow_____," Frank Zappa
8. "The Little White_____That Cried," Johnny Ray
9. "Don't Let the_____Go Down on Me," Elton John (extra credit for the best wrong answer!)
10. "_____the People," James Taylor

See page 95 for answers.

THE IVY LEAGUE ROCK AND ROLL QUIZ BOOK

WILL THE **REAL** BALDEMAR HUERTA PLEASE STAND UP?

Match the performer with his real name:

- **A.** Ringo Starr
- **B.** Rick James
- **C.** Elvis Costello
- **D.** Freddy Fender
- **E.** Alice Cooper
- **F.** Cat Stevens
- **G.** Elton John
- **H.** Meat Loaf
- **I.** John Denver
- **J.** ? (Question Mark)
- **K.** Muddy Waters
- **L.** Tiny Tim
- **M.** Bob Dylan

- **1.** Declan McManus
- **2.** Vincent Furnier
- **3.** Baldemar Huerta
- **4.** Henry Deutschendorf
- **5.** Marvin Lee Aday
- **6.** McKinley Morganfield
- **7.** Reg Dwight
- **8.** Richard Starkey
- **9.** James Johnson
- **10.** Robert Zimmerman
- **11.** Rudy Martinez
- **12.** Stephen Demetri Georgiou
- **13.** Herbert Buckingham Khaury

See page 95 for answers.

THE IVY LEAGUE ROCK AND ROLL QUIZ BOOK

HELLO, IT'S ME

Identify this artist's first album (U.S. versions only).

1. **Frank Zappa and the Mothers of Invention**
    a. *Freak Out!*
    b. *Absolutely Free*
    c. *The Grand Wazoo*
    d. *Cruising: With Ruben and the Jets*

2. **Billy Joel:**
    a. *Piano Man*
    b. *Streetlife Serenade*
    c. *Cold Spring Harbor*
    d. *Billy Joel*

3. **Elvis Costello:**
    a. *Alison*
    b. *My Aim is True*
    c. *Armed Forces*
    d. *This Year's Model*

4. **Jethro Tull:**
    a. *Stand Up*
    b. *Thick As A Brick*
    c. *This Was*
    d. *Flute of the Room*

5. **Bruce Springsteen:**
    a. *Born to Run*
    b. *Greetings From Asbury Park, N.J.*
    c. *Blinded by the Light*
    d. *The Wild, the Innocent and the E Street Shuffle*

THE IVY LEAGUE ROCK AND ROLL QUIZ BOOK
HELLO, IT'S ME

6. **The Grateful Dead:**
    a. *The Grateful Dead*
    b. *Aoxomoxoa*
    c. *American Beauty*
    d. *Born to Be Dead*

7. **The Police:**
    a. *Regatta de Blanc*
    b. *Zenyatta Mondatta*
    c. *Outlandos D'Amour*
    d. *Magilla Gorilla*

8. **The Beatles:**
    a. *Meet the Beatles!*
    b. *The Beatles*
    c. *The Beatles, England's Newest Hitmakers*
    d. *We're Gonna Change the Face of Pop Music Forever*

9. **Jimi Hendrix:**
    a. *Electric Ladyland*
    b. *Voodoo Chile*
    c. *Cry of Love*
    d. *Are You Experienced?*

10. **Simon and Garfunkel:**
    a. *The Sounds of Silence*
    b. *Parsley, Sage, Rosemary and Thyme*
    c. *Wednesday Morning, 3 A.M.*
    d. *A Poem on the Underground Wall*

See page 96 for answers.

I WRITE THE SONGS

Each of these hits was penned by a famous performer who was not a member of the group or the individual artist that made the song popular. Who were these songwriters?

1. "I'm a Believer," The Monkees
2. "Woodstock," Crosby, Stills, Nash & Young
3. "This Masquerade," George Benson
4. "It's All Over Now," The Rolling Stones
5. "My Way," Frank Sinatra
6. "Hello, Mary Lou," Rick Nelson
7. "The First Cut Is The Deepest," Rod Stewart
8. "This Little Girl," Gary U.S. Bonds
9. "The Mighty Quinn," Manfred Mann
10. "Love Will Keep Us Together," The Captain and Tennille
11. "All The Young Dudes," Mott The Hoople
12. "You've Got a Friend," James Taylor
13. "Mama Told Me Not To Come," Three Dog Night
14. "Lotta Love," Nicolette Larson
15. "Stoney End," Barbra Streisand

See page 97 for answers.

THE IVY LEAGUE ROCK AND ROLL QUIZ BOOK

YOU CAN ALL JOIN IN

Who is the guest star playing this instrument on this song?

1. Guitar on "While My Guitar Gently Weeps," The Beatles
2. Saxophone on "Walk On The Wild Side," Lou Reed
3. Guitar on "You Really Got Me," The Kinks
4. Saxophone on "Urgent," Foreigner
5. Vocals on "Hungry Heart," Bruce Springsteen
6. Piano on "Revolution," The Beatles
7. Guitar on "On Broadway," The Drifters
8. Drums on "Will You Love Me Tomorrow," The Shirelles
9. Vocals on "You're So Vain," Carly Simon
10. Organ on "Let It Be," The Beatles
11. Guitar on "Badge," Cream
12. Drums on "Please, Mr. Postman," The Marvelettes
13. Keyboards on "Whatever Gets You Through the Night," John Lennon
14. Guitar on "Layla," Derek and the Dominoes
15. Vocals on "Tempted," Squeeze

See page 98 for answers.

THE IVY LEAGUE ROCK AND ROLL QUIZ BOOK
MASS PRODUCTION

Each of these albums was produced by another noteworthy performer. Match the album and the producer.

1. *Pussy Cats,* Harry Nilsson
2. *Hollywood Dream,* Thunderclap Newman
3. *We're An American Band,* Grand Funk Railroad
4. *Wild Gift,* X
5. *Armed Forces,* Elvis Costello
6. *Transformer,* Lou Reed
7. *Drop Down & Get Me,* Del Shannon
8. *Beautiful Noise,* Neil Diamond
9. *East Side Story,* Squeeze
10. *Guilty,* Barbra Streisand

A. Nick Lowe
B. Tom Petty
C. Barry Gibb
D. John Lennon
E. David Bowie
F. Pete Townshend
G. Robbie Robertson
H. Todd Rundgren
I. Elvis Costello
J. Ray Manzarek

See page 98 for answers.

THE IVY LEAGUE ROCK AND ROLL QUIZ BOOK

MYSTERY ROCK STAR #2

This is the little boy who would be King.

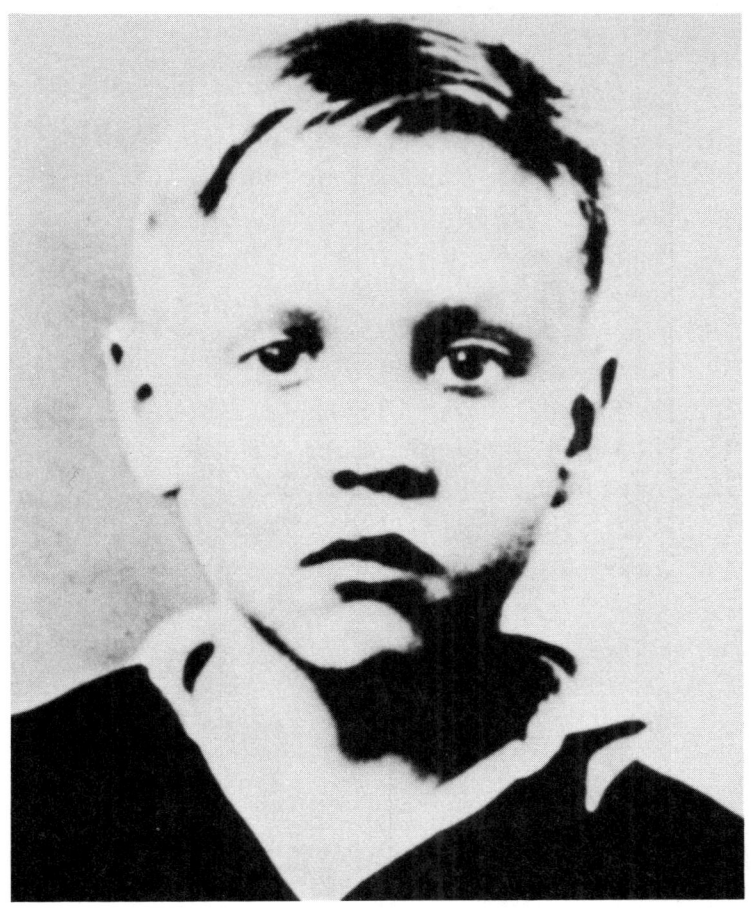

See page 142 for answers.

THE IVY LEAGUE ROCK AND ROLL QUIZ BOOK
ALL BY MYSELF

Which present or former member of this band recorded this solo album?

1. The Rolling Stones, *I've Got My Own Album To Do*
2. The Eagles, *But Seriously, Folks*
3. The Who, *Smash Your Head Against the Wall*
4. Black Sabbath, *Diary of a Madman*
5. Yes, *Olias of Sunhillow*
6. The Beatles, *Extra Texture*
7. Genesis, *Face Value*
8. Jefferson Airplane, *Welcome to the Wrecking Ball*
9. The Steve Miller Band, *Silk Degrees*
10. The Faces, *Gasoline Alley*
11. The Velvet Underground, *Street Hassle*
12. Roxy Music, *Another Green World*
13. Talking Heads, *Songs From "The Catherine Wheel"*
14. Traffic, *Arc of a Diver*

See page 100 for answers.

? ? ? ? ? ? ? ?

THE IVY LEAGUE ROCK AND ROLL QUIZ BOOK
HOT SPACES

Some song titles only tell half the story. Fill in the parentheses that are part of these song titles.

1. "(   ) Close To You," The Carpenters
2. "Alone Again (   )," Gilbert O'Sullivan
3. "(   ) I'm Losing You," The Temptations
4. "I Never Loved A Man (   )," Aretha Franklin
5. "(   ) Satisfaction," The Rolling Stones
6. "I Want You (   )," James Brown
7. "Master Blaster (   )," Stevie Wonder
8. "(   ) Red Shoes," Elvis Costello
9. "Norwegian Wood (   )," The Beatles
10. "It's My Party (   )," Lesley Gore
11. "(   ) Higher and Higher," Jackie Wilson
12. "It's Alright, Ma (   )," Bob Dylan
13. "Would You Lay With Me (   )" Tanya Tucker
14. "(   ) Superman," The Kinks
15. "Take Me In Your Arms (   )," The Isley Brothers

See page 100 for answers.

? ? ? ? ? ? ? ?

THE IVY LEAGUE ROCK AND ROLL QUIZ BOOK

SHE'S A WOMAN

Name the woman missing from each song title.

1. "Suite:_____ Blue Eyes," Crosby, Stills, & Nash
2. "Absolutely Sweet_____ ," Bob Dylan
3. "For_____ , Wherever I May Find Her," Simon & Garfunkel
4. "Sweet_____ ," The Velvet Underground
5. "Long Tall_____ ," Little Richard
6. "_____ Darling," Bruce Springsteen
7. "_____ Smile," Hall & Oates
8. "All For_____ ," Billy Joel
9. "_____ Don't Lose That Number," Steely Dan
10. "Help Me,_____ ," The Beach Boys

See page 101 for answers.

MEANINGLESS BUT TRUE

Who performed the song with the nonsense title?

1. "Da Doo Ron Ron"
2. "Shimmy Shimmy Ko Ko Bop"
3. "Do Wah Diddy Diddy"
4. "De Do Do Do, De Da Da Da"
5. "Yakety Yak"
6. "In-A-Gadda-Da-Vida"
7. "Be-Bop-A-Lula"
8. "Ya Ya"
9. "Ob-la-di, Ob-la-da"
10. "Boogie Oogie Oogie"

See page 101 for answers.

THE IVY LEAGUE ROCK AND ROLL QUIZ BOOK
I GOT A WOMAN

What is the name of the woman mentioned in this song?

1. "Born to Run," Bruce Springsteen
2. "Only the Good Die Young," Billy Joel
3. "America," Simon & Garfunkel
4. "Superwoman," Stevie Wonder
5. "Crocodile Rock," Elton John
6. "Fire and Rain," James Taylor
7. "Let It Be," The Beatles
8. "Daydream Believer," The Monkees
9. "Stay With Me," The Faces
10. "Baba O'Riley," The Who

See page 102 for answers.

THE IVY LEAGUE ROCK AND ROLL QUIZ BOOK

UNDER THE COVERS

The expression "cover" is music industry jargon for a version of someone else's song. What was the hit song covered by these performers?

A. Little Eva, Grand Funk Railroad
B. Roy Orbison, Van Halen
C. Tommy James and the Shondells, Joan Jett and the Blackhearts
D. Sam Cooke, Art Garfunkel
E. The Tokens, Robert John
F. Jackie Wilson, Rita Coolidge
G. Johnny Burnette, Ringo Starr
H. Chuck Berry, The Electric Light Orchestra
I. The Crystals, Shaun Cassidy
J. The Righteous Brothers, Hall & Oates
K. The Jackson 5, Gloria Gaynor
L. Richard Harris, Waylon Jennings, Donna Summer
M. Sam and Dave, The Blues Brothers

UNDER THE COVERS

Here's the hit cover—who had the original hit?

- **N.** "Angel of the Morning," Juice Newton
- **O.** "That'll Be the Day," Linda Ronstadt
- **P.** "Blinded by the Light," Manfred Mann's Earth Band
- **Q.** "Why Do Fools Fall in Love," Diana Ross
- **R.** "Stay," The Four Seasons, Jackson Browne
- **S.** "I Shot the Sheriff," Eric Clapton
- **T.** "Crying," Don McLean
- **U.** "Take Me to the River," The Talking Heads
- **V.** "The Night They Drove Old Dixie Down," Joan Baez
- **W.** "Handy Man," James Taylor
- **X.** "One Fine Day," Carole King
- **Y.** "Hooked on a Feeling," Blue Swede
- **Z.** "Land of a Thousand Dances," Wilson Pickett

See page 102 for answers.

THE IVY LEAGUE ROCK AND ROLL QUIZ BOOK

MYSTERY ROCK STAR #3

She's our little rock and roll.

See page 142 for answers.

THE IVY LEAGUE ROCK AND ROLL QUIZ BOOK

THE MAN IN THE GLASS BOOTH

Since the heyday of the legendary Phil Spector who produced The Crystals, The Ronettes, The Righteous Brothers, top-ranked record producers have become superstars themselves. Match these albums with their producers.

1. *Tug of War,* Paul McCartney
2. *End of the Century,* The Ramones
3. *No Secrets,* Carly Simon
4. *Candy-O,* The Cars
5. *Sticky Fingers,* The Rolling Stones
6. *Who's Next,* The Who
7. *Blonde on Blonde,* Bob Dylan
8. *Glass Houses,* Billy Joel
9. *The Velvet Underground & Nico,* The Velvet Underground
10. *Dark Side of the Moon,* Pink Floyd

A. Glyn Johns
B. Alan Parsons
C. Bob Johnston
D. Phil Spector
E. Roy Thomas Baker
F. Andy Warhol
G. George Martin
H. Richard Perry
I. Phil Ramone
J. Jimmy Miller

See page 104 for answers.

THE IVY LEAGUE ROCK AND ROLL QUIZ BOOK

ONE PILL MAKES YOU LARGER...

Which of these 1960's groups had these psychedelic hits? (All of these groups really existed!)

1. "White Rabbit":
   - a. Moby Grape
   - b. Jefferson Airplane
   - c. The Charging Tyrannosaurus of Despair

2. "I Had Too Much to Dream Last Night":
   - a. The Electric Prunes
   - b. It's A Beautiful Day
   - c. The Peanut Butter Conspiracy

3. "Lucy In the Sky With Diamonds":
   - a. Eric Burdon and the Animals
   - b. The Moody Blues
   - c. The Beatles

4. "Purple Haze":
   - a. The Jimi Hendrix Experience
   - b. Santana
   - c. Lothar and the Hand People

5. "Eight Miles High":
   - a. The Grateful Dead
   - b. The Hollies
   - c. The Byrds

THE IVY LEAGUE ROCK AND ROLL QUIZ BOOK
ONE PILL MAKES YOU LARGER...

6. **"American Woman":**
    a. *The Guess Who*
    b. *The Strawberry Alarm Clock*
    c. *Yes*

7. **"Question":**
    a. *The Remains*
    b. *The Moody Blues*
    c. *Cream*

8. **"Mellow Yellow":**
    a. *The Holy Modal Rounders*
    b. *The Magic Mushrooms*
    c. *Donovan*

9. **"Ichycoo Park":**
    a. *The Small Faces*
    b. *The 13th Floor Elevators*
    c. *The Only Alternative and His Other Possibilities*

10. **"2000 Light Years From Home":**
    a. *Country Joe and the Fish*
    b. *The Incredible String Band*
    c. *The Rolling Stones*

See page 105 for answers.

THE IVY LEAGUE ROCK AND ROLL QUIZ BOOK

TAKING CARE OF BUSINESS

After the legendary royalty rip-offs of the '50s and '60s, musicians realized that they had to take control of the publishing end of their songs—and thus of their rightful profits. By the mid-'70s, it was nearly as common for a performer to own his own publishing company as it was to own his own amplifier. Match these writer-performers with their whimsically named publishing companies.

1. Ian Anderson of Jethro Tull
2. Elvis Costello
3. Bob Dylan
4. Joni Mitchell
5. Van Morrison
6. Jimmy Page & Robert Plant of Led Zeppelin
7. Bob Seger
8. James Taylor
9. Pete Townshend of The Who
10. Stevie Wonder

A. Black Bull Music
B. Caledonia Soul Music
C. Crazy Crow Music
D. Country Road Music
E. Dwarf Music
F. Gear Music
G. Fabulous Music
H. Plangent Visions Music
I. Salamander & Son Music
J. Superhype Music

See page 105 for answers.

THE IVY LEAGUE ROCK AND ROLL QUIZ BOOK

WORDS OF LOVE

Each of these songs was covered by the Beatles. Who were the original artists?

1. "Matchbox"
2. "Roll Over Beethoven"
3. "Words of Love"
4. "Money (That's What I Want)"
5. "Act Naturally"
6. "Dizzy Miss Lizzie"
7. "Long Tall Sally"
8. "Twist and Shout"
9. "Baby It's You"
10. "Please Mr. Postman"

See page 106 for answers.

GET IT RIGHT THE FIRST TIME

Each of these songs is commonly referred to by an incorrect name—usually the first line of the chorus. What is the real name of each song?

1. "Rolling On The River," Creedence Clearwater Revival
2. "Everybody Must Get Stoned," Bob Dylan
3. "Teenage Wasteland," The Who
4. "Feelin' Groovy," Simon & Garfunkel
5. "Rust Never Sleeps," Neil Young
6. "Go Ask Alice," Jefferson Airplane
7. "What's That Sound?" Buffalo Springfield
8. "She's My Little Rock and Roll," The Rolling Stones
9. "Ground Control to Major Tom," David Bowie
10. "When Will I Hold You Again," Barry White

See page 107 for answers.

THE IVY LEAGUE ROCK AND ROLL QUIZ BOOK

WE GOTTA GET OUT OF THIS PLACE

Match the star with his previous occupation:

- **A.** Elvis Presley
- **B.** Roger Daltrey
- **C.** Jimi Hendrix
- **D.** Ian Dury
- **E.** Chuck Berry
- **F.** Chrissie Hynde
- **G.** Rod Stewart
- **H.** Elvis Costello
- **I.** Deborah Harry
- **J.** Sly Stone
- **K.** Grace Slick
- **L.** Chubby Checker

1. Model
2. Gravedigger
3. Beautician
4. Computer Programmer
5. Paratrooper
6. Truck Driver
7. Chicken Plucker
8. Rock Critic
9. Disc Jockey
10. Sheet Metal Worker
11. Playboy bunny
12. College Professor

Match the star with his or her alma mater:

- **M.** Neil Diamond
- **N.** Mick Jagger
- **O.** Carly Simon
- **P.** Jim Morrison
- **Q.** David Byrne
- **R.** Grace Slick
- **S.** Paul Simon
- **T.** Gram Parsons

13. UCLA
14. Sarah Lawrence College
15. Queens College
16. London School of Economics
17. Finch College
18. New York University
19. Rhode Island School of Design
20. Harvard University

See page 108 for answers.

BODY LANGUAGE

Drag out your old anatomy textbook and complete these song titles with the appropriate body parts.

1. "Bette Davis _____," Kim Carnes
2. "Our _____ Are Sealed," The Go-Gos
3. "Stop Dragging My _____ Around," Stevie Nicks
4. "Sunshine on My _____," John Denver
5. "_____ —Part 2," Little Stevie Wonder
6. "Hot _____," Rod Stewart
7. "Under My _____," The Rolling Stones
8. "I Want To Hold Your _____," The Beatles
9. "The First Time Ever I Saw Your _____," Roberta Flack
10. "Over My _____," Fleetwood Mac

See page 108 for answers.

THE IVY LEAGUE ROCK AND ROLL QUIZ BOOK
GET TOGETHER

Name these one-time duets or collaborations:

1. David Bowie & Queen
2. Barbra Streisand & Donna Summer
3. Elton John & Kiki Dee
4. Paul Simon & Phoebe Snow
5. Stevie Wonder & Paul McCartney
6. Bob and Doug McKenzie & Geddy Lee
7. Neil Diamond & Barbra Streisand
8. David Bowie & John Lennon
9. The Rolling Stones & Merry Clayton
10. George Harrison, Ringo Starr, & Paul and Linda McCartney

EXTRA CREDIT: *There is a Beatles song on which the Rolling Stones sing back-up, and a Rolling Stones song on which the Beatles sing back-up. What are they?*

See page 109 for answers.

MYSTERY ROCK STAR #4

Back when this picture was taken, the be-hatted babe was <u>scolded</u> for putting strange things in his mouth!

See page 142 for answers.

THE IVY LEAGUE ROCK AND ROLL QUIZ BOOK

LEADER OF THE PACK

Identify the band for which this person sang the lead:

1. Keith Relf
2. John Kaye
3. Paul Jones
4. Jon Anderson
5. Ronnie Van Zant
6. Phil Lynott
7. Lou Gramm
8. Eric Bloom
9. Joe Strummer
10. Geddy Lee
11. Mick Jagger
12. Kevin Cronin
13. David Byrne
14. Jim Morrison
15. Burton Cummings

See page 110 for answers.

PACK OF THE LEADER

Identify the lead singer of this band:

1. The Pretenders
2. Cheap Trick
3. Creedence Clearwater Revival
4. The Police
5. The Kinks
6. The J. Geils Band
7. The Who
8. Van Halen
9. Boston
10. Herman's Hermits
11. Led Zeppelin
12. The Lovin' Spoonful
13. Big Brother and the Holding Company
14. Humble Pie
15. Bad Company

See page 111 for answers.

THE IVY LEAGUE ROCK AND ROLL QUIZ BOOK
MY LITTLE TOWN

These groups of bands and performers each share a single city for a home base. Identify the cities.

1. The M C 5, Ted Nugent, The Stooges, Bob Seger
2. The Cars, The J.Geils Band, The Modern Lovers, The Ultimate Spinach
3. Creedence Clearwater Revival, Jefferson Airplane, Moby Grape, The Residents
4. Blondie, The Ramones, The Shangri-Las, The Velvet Underground
5. The Beach Boys, Black Flag, The Doors, The Eagles
6. Fats Domino, Lee Dorsey, Dr. John the Night Tripper, The Meters
7. The Bar-Kays, Booker T and the MGs, Elvis Presley, Rufus Thomas
8. Chubby Checker, Fabian, Harold Melvin & the Blue Notes, The O'Jays
9. The Paul Butterfield Blues Band, Howlin' Wolf, The Impressions, Styx
10. The Clash, The Kinks, Pink Floyd, The Who

See page 112 for answers.

THE IVY LEAGUE ROCK AND ROLL QUIZ BOOK
LONDON CALLING

Which groups of the British Invasion made these songs U.S. hits?

1. "Go Now"
    a. *Wayne Fontana and the Mindbenders*
    b. *Peter and Gordon*
    c. *The Moody Blues*

2. "Ferry Cross the Mersey"
    a. *Chad and Jeremy*
    b. *The Animals*
    c. *Gerry and the Pacemakers*

3. "Bad to Me"
    a. *Herman's Hermits*
    b. *Billy J. Kramer and the Dakotas*
    c. *The Swinging Blue Jeans*

4. "She's Not There"
    a. *The Zombies*
    b. *Freddie and the Dreamers*
    c. *The Yardbirds*

5. "Glad All Over"
    a. *The Dave Clark Five*
    b. *Manfred Mann*
    c. *The Kinks*

6. "World Without Love"
    a. *Peter and Gordon*
    b. *Chad and Jeremy*
    c. *Georgie Fame and the Blue Flames*

THE IVY LEAGUE ROCK AND ROLL QUIZ BOOK
LONDON CALLING

7. "Mrs. Brown, You've Got A Lovely Daughter"
   a. *Gerry and the Pacemakers*
   b. *The Nashville Teens*
   c. *Herman's Hermits*

8. "Can't Buy Me Love":
   a. *The Hollies*
   b. *The Beatles*
   c. *Them*

9. "I'm Telling You Now"
   a. *The Moody Blues*
   b. *The Dave Clark Five*
   c. *Freddie and the Dreamers*

10. "You Really Got Me"
    a. *The Beatles*
    b. *The Rolling Stones*
    c. *The Kinks*

See page 112 for answers.

45

THE IVY LEAGUE ROCK AND ROLL QUIZ BOOK

WITH A LITTLE HELP FROM MY FRIENDS

Here is the back-up band. Who are the singers they support?

1. The Attractions
2. The Four Seasons
3. The Crickets
4. The Heartbreakers
5. The Famous Flames
6. The E Street Band
7. The Teenagers
8. The Shondells
9. The Harlettes
10. The Wailers

The flip side: Here is the singer. What are the back-up bands?

11. Joan Jett
12. Cliff Richard
13. Billy J. Kramer
14. Robin Lane
15. Johnny Cash
16. Bob Seger
17. Mitch Ryder
18. Smokey Robinson
19. Huey Lewis
20. Jonathan Richman

See page 113 for answers.

THE IVY LEAGUE ROCK AND ROLL QUIZ BOOK

A NIGHT AT THE OPERA

In the liner notes to Todd Rundgren's *Something/Anything?* (1972), the artist explains that he "drafted the songs into a kind of pop operetta, that kind of thing being very popular nowadays." It sure was—here's a sampling from the Album Age. Who performed these rock operas and song cycles?

1. *S.F. Sorrow*
2. *Tommy*
3. *The Wall*
4. *Berlin*
5. *Joe's Garage*
6. *Preservation*
7. *Keynsham*
8. *Numbers*
9. *Good Old Boys*
10. *A Passion Play*

See page 114 for answers.

TWO FOR THE SHOW

Which of these albums is a double (two records)?

1. *Quadrophenia,* The Who
2. *London Calling,* The Clash
3. *Live at Budokan,* Cheap Trick
4. *Physical Graffiti,* Led Zeppelin
5. *Chicago IX,* Chicago
6. *Welcome Back, My Friends, to the Show That Never Ends,* Emerson, Lake, and Palmer
7. *The River,* Bruce Springsteen
8. *Paradise Theater,* Styx
9. *A Night at the Opera,* Queen
10. *Out of the Blue,* Electric Light Orchestra

See page 114 for answers.

THE IVY LEAGUE ROCK AND ROLL QUIZ BOOK
FREEZE-FRAME

Which rock group or singer starred in this film?

1. *Caveman*
2. *Having A Wild Weekend*
3. *Journey Through The Past*
4. *The Song Remains The Same*
5. *200 Motels*
6. *Change of Habit*
7. *The Man Who Fell To Earth*
8. *The Great Rock 'n' Roll Swindle*
9. *Rude Boy*
10. *Renaldo & Clara*
11. *One-Trick Pony*
12. *Union City*
13. *Gimme Shelter*
14. *All You Need Is Cash*
15. *The Harder They Come*
16. *Two-Lane Blacktop*
17. *Rock 'n' Roll High School*
18. *The Fastest Guitar Alive*
19. *The Rose*
20. *Head*

See page 116 for answers.

THE IVY LEAGUE ROCK AND ROLL QUIZ BOOK

MYSTERY ROCK STAR #5

Even at the tender age of four, this future superstar was looking very sexy!

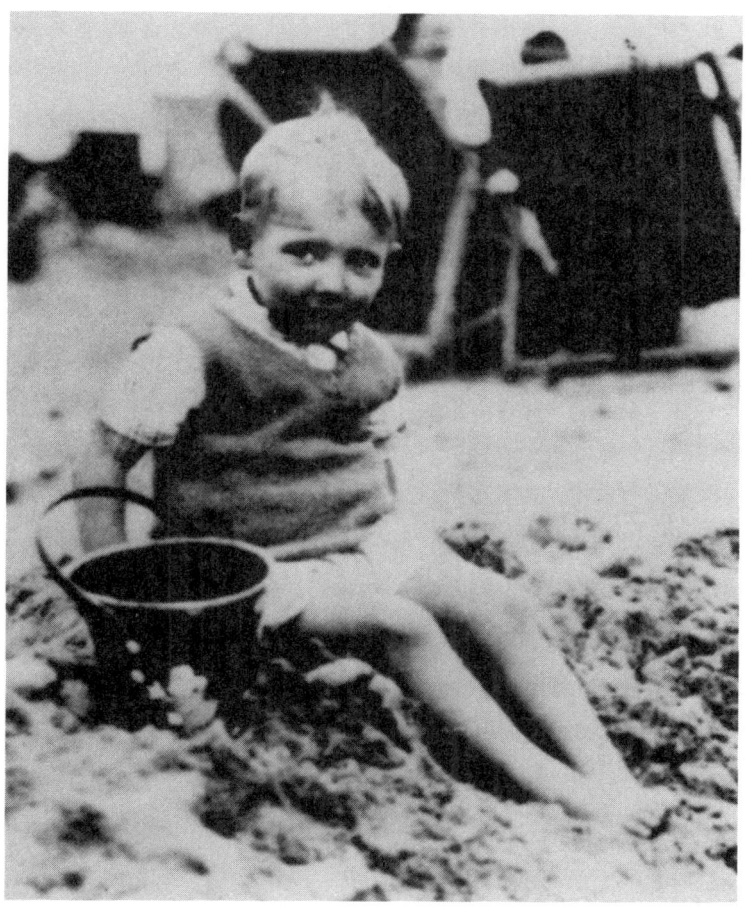

See page 142 for answers.

THE IVY LEAGUE ROCK AND ROLL QUIZ BOOK
CELLULOID HEROES

The two medias of rock music and film overlap constantly. Each of these hits made its first appearance in a movie—which movie was it?

A. "Nobody Does It Better," Carly Simon
B. "Last Dance," Donna Summer
C. "Stayin' Alive," The Bee Gees
D. "Raindrops Keep Fallin' On My Head," B.J. Thomas
E. "Late in the Evening," Paul Simon
F. "Eye of the Tiger," Survivor
G. "Knockin' On Heaven's Door," Bob Dylan
H. "Call Me," Blondie
I. "Mrs. Robinson," Simon & Garfunkel
J. "Evergreen," Barbra Streisand

On the flip side: Who performed these title songs?

K. "Live and Let Die"
L. "Endless Love"
M. "The Main Event"
N. "Grease"
O. "Super Fly"
P. "9 to 5"
Q. "Chariots of Fire"
R. "The Goodbye Girl"
S. "That's the Way of the World"
T. "High School Confidential"

See page 118 for answers.

SLEEPING WITH THE TELEVISION ON

Match the TV show theme with the performer who took it to the Top 40.

1. "Hawaii Five-O"
2. "Theme From SWAT"
3. "The Rockford Files"
4. "Welcome Back (Kotter)"
5. "Happy Days"
6. "Keep Your Eye on the Sparrow" (theme from Barretta)
7. "Twilight Zone"
8. "Peter Gunn"
9. "Secret Agent Man"
10. "Hill Street Blues"

A. Mike Post
B. Henry Mancini
C. The Manhattan Transfer
D. Rhythm Heritage
E. Pratt and McClain
F. The Ventures
G. Johnny Rivers
H. John Sebastian
I. Sammy Davis, Jr.
J. Mike Post again

See page 119 for answers.

THE IVY LEAGUE ROCK AND ROLL QUIZ BOOK

IT'S ALIVE

What band or performer recorded this concert album?

1. *Rock and Roll Animal*
2. *Kick Out the Jams*
3. *Live At Leeds*
4. *Rock of Ages*
5. *Welcome Back, My Friends, to the Show That Never Ends*
6. *Bursting Out*
7. *Still Life*
8. *Time Fades Away*
9. *Absolutely Live*
10. *Bless Its Pointed Little Head*
11. *Some Enchanted Evening*
12. *Made in Japan*
13. *Shadows and Light*
14. *One For the Road*
15. *Stand in the Fire*

See page 119 for answers.

ROCKER MORTIS

What caused the deaths of these young rockers?

1. Duane Allman
2. Harry Chapin
3. Johnny Ace
4. Sam Cooke
5. Brian Jones
6. Buddy Holly
7. Donny Hathaway
8. Janis Joplin
9. Cass Elliott
10. Jim Morrison

See page 120 for answers.

THE IVY LEAGUE ROCK AND ROLL QUIZ BOOK
SELLING OUT

Match the hit with the product it was corrupted to advertise:

1. "California Girls," The Beach Boys
2. "Calendar Girl," Neil Sedaka
3. "Whole Lotta Shakin' Goin On," Jerry Lee Lewis
4. "Light My Fire," The Doors
5. "Anticipation," Carly Simon
6. "Good Vibrations," The Beach Boys
7. "Oh, Pretty Woman," Roy Orbison
8. "The Candy Man," Sammy Davis, Jr.
9. "The Twist," Chubby Checker
10. "Short Shorts," The Royal Teens
11. "Yummy Yummy Yummy," Ohio Express
12. "Up, Up, & Away," The Fifth Dimension
13. "Just One Look," Doris Troy
14. "Still The One," Orleans

A. ABC Television
B. Heinz Ketchup
C. Shakey's Pizza
D. Esskay Meats
E. TWA (Trans World Airlines)
F. Clairol Herbal Essence Shampoo
G. Mazda
H. Sunkist
I. Tone Soap
J. M&Ms
K. Purina Cat Chow
L. Brim Coffee
M. Buick
N. Nair

EXTRA CREDIT: *What hit song was originally a Coca-Cola commercial before its successful recording by the New Seekers?*

See page 121 for answers.

THE IVY LEAGUE ROCK AND ROLL QUIZ BOOK
YOU'RE ENTITLED

Fill in the missing word in this song title.

1. "Please _____ Postman," The Marvelettes
2. "_____ Jane Approximately," Bob Dylan
3. "_____ of the Road," Roger Miller
4. "_____ of Earl," Gene Chandler
5. "I _____ the Tears," The Drifters
6. "_____ Robinson," Simon and Garfunkel
7. "Good Golly _____ Molly," Little Richard
8. "Calling _____ Love," KISS
9. "_____ Idaho," The B-52s
10. "I'm Your _____," Grand Funk Railroad

See page 122 for answers.

I CALL YOUR NAME

Which of these bands are not named after a member of the band?

1. Alice Cooper
2. Jethro Tull
3. Uriah Heep
4. Manfred Mann
5. The J. Geils Band
6. The Marshall Tucker Band
7. Tommy Tutone
8. Lynyrd Skynyrd
9. Fanny
10. Van Halen

See page 122 for answers.

THE IVY LEAGUE ROCK AND ROLL QUIZ BOOK

MYSTERY ROCK STAR #6

These three little prodigies became responsible for a fever that swept the nation!

See page 142 for answers.

THE IVY LEAGUE ROCK AND ROLL QUIZ BOOK
ON THE ROAD

Complete each street-wise song title.

1. "Dancing in the _____," Martha and the Vandellas
2. "Creeque _____," The Mamas and the Papas
3. "Thunder _____," Bruce Springsteen
4. "Penny _____," The Beatles
5. "In the _____ of the Crimson King," King Crimson
6. "Cypress _____," Van Morrison
7. "_____ to Hell," AC/DC
8. "Under the _____," The Drifters
9. "Nights on _____," The Bee Gees
10. "Desolation _____," Bob Dylan

See page 123 for answers.

I LOVE ROCK AND ROLL

Who performed these rock anthems? (Original artists, please.)

1. "Long Live Rock"
2. "Rock and Roll Music"
3. "It's Still Rock and Roll to Me"
4. "I Love Rock and Roll"
5. "It Will Stand"
6. "Rock and Roll Never Forgets"
7. "Rock and Roll is Here to Stay"
8. "Rock Around the Clock"
9. "Do You Believe in Magic"
10. "All the Way From Memphis"

See page 124 for answers.

THE IVY LEAGUE ROCK AND ROLL QUIZ BOOK
OFF THE RECORD

What was unusual about the sleeves of these albums?

1. *The Beatles,* The Beatles
2. *In Through the Out Door,* Led Zeppelin
3. *E Pluribus Funk,* Grand Funk Railroad
4. *Lace and Whiskey,* Alice Cooper
5. *Stand Up,* Jethro Tull
6. *Ooh La La,* The Faces
7. *The Velvet Underground & Nico* (first editions)
8. *Sticky Fingers,* The Rolling Stones
9. *Their Satanic Majesties Request,* The Rolling Stones (first editions)
10. *Talking Book,* Stevie Wonder (first editions)

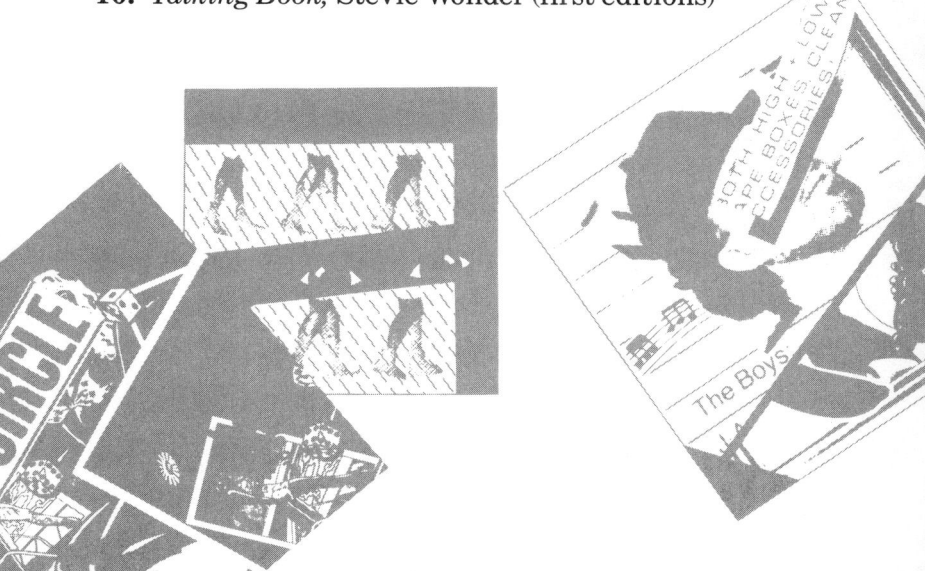

See page 125 for answers.

ONE-HIT WONDERS

The Ivy League Rock and Roll Quiz Book

Every rock season contains its share of one-hit wonders, artists unwilling or unable to follow up their one big success. Here is the song—name the artist whose only U.S. Top 40 hit it was.

A. "Kung Fu Fighting"
B. "Green Tambourine"
C. "Incense and Peppermints"
D. "Alley-Oop"
E. "Funkytown"
F. "Pop Muzik"
G. "Judy in Disguise With Glasses"
H. "In-A-Gadda-Da-Vida"
I. "Something in the Air"
J. "Chuck E.'s in Love"
K. "I Do the Rock"
L. "Don't Give Up on Us, Baby"
M. "Disco Duck"
N. "Monster Mash"
O. "In the Year 2525"
P. "Come Go With Me"
Q. "Eve of Destruction"
R. "Afternoon Delight"
S. "Psychotic Reaction"
T. "You Light Up My Life"
U. "Sweet City Woman"
V. "The Boys Are Back in Town"
W. "Get Together"
X. "Play That Funky Music (White Boy)"
Y. "Talk Talk"
Z. "Game of Love"

See page 126 for answers.

THE IVY LEAGUE ROCK AND ROLL QUIZ BOOK

I FOUGHT THE LAW

Each of these performers went to prison, serving sentences that ranged from long to very short. Match the artist with the charge that put him behind bars.

1. Chuck Berry
2. Chuck Berry (second conviction)
3. Arlo Guthrie
4. Chrissie Hynde
5. Paul McCartney
6. Phil Ochs
7. Sid Vicious
8. Mick Jagger and Keith Richards
9. Wendy O. Williams
10. Little Willie John

A. Drunkeness and disorderly conduct
B. Possesssion of drugs
C. Vagrancy
D. Violation of the Mann Act—transporting girls across state lines for immortal porpoises—uh, immoral purposes
E. Murder
F. Onstage obscenity and resisting arrest
G. Possession of marijuana
H. Tax evasion
I. Manslaughter
J. Littering

See page 128 for answers.

THE IVY LEAGUE ROCK AND ROLL QUIZ BOOK

MYSTERY ROCK STAR #7

This cool cat grew up to enjoy two careers; a video doctor and a rocker par exellence!

See page 142 for answers.

COMBAT ROCK

Which New Wave Groups released these albums?

1. London Calling
2. Under the Big Black Sun
3. Rocket to Russia
4. Ghost in the Machine
5. Marquee Moon
6. Parallel Lines
7. More Songs About Buildings and Food
8. Duty Now for the Future
9. Beyond the Valley of 1983
10. Solid Gold

A. Talking Heads
B. X
C. The gang of Four
D. Television
E. The Clash
F. The Police
G. The Plasmatics
H. The Ramones
I. Devo
J. Blondie

See page 129 for answers.

ROCKIN' ALL OVER THE WORLD

What country do each of these bands hail from?

1. AC/DC
2. ABBA
3. Kraftwerk
4. The Plastics
5. Devo
6. Rush
7. Golden Earring
8. Toots and the Maytals
9. Thin Lizzy
10. The Rolling Stones

See page 129 for answers.

THE IVY LEAGUE ROCK AND ROLL QUIZ BOOK
POINT OF ORDER

Arrange these Beatles albums (US versions) in order of release.

1. *The Beatles*
2. *A Hard Day's Night*
3. *Meet the Beatles!*
4. *Rubber Soul*
5. *Yellow Submarine*
6. *Revolver*
7. *The Beatles Story*
8. *Beatles '65*
9. *Let It Be*
10. *Sgt. Pepper's Lonely Hearts Club Band*
11. *"Yesterday" . . . and Today*
12. *Help!*
13. *Something Old Something New*
14. *Abbey Road*
15. *The Beatles' Second Album*
16. *Hey Jude*
17. *Magical Mystery Tour*

See page 130 for answers.

THE IVY LEAGUE ROCK AND ROLL QUIZ BOOK

WHERE I'M COMING FROM

In keeping with tradition, each of these rockers paid his dues before making it big. Match the soon-to-be star with his or her old band.

1. Bruce Springsteen
2. Rick Springfield
3. Ian Dury
4. Todd Rundgren
5. Billy Joel
6. Deborah Harry
7. Rod Stewart
8. Ted Nugent
9. Van Morrison
10. Grace Slick
11. Robert Plant
12. Elton John
13. Linda Ronstadt
14. Steve Winwood
15. Peter Frampton
16. Janis Joplin
17. Wilson Pickett
18. Maria Muldaur
19. Kenny Rogers
20. Christine McVie

A. Band of Joy
B. The Amboy Dukes
C. The Falcons
D. The Stone Poneys
E. Dr. Zoom and his Sonic Boom
F. The Hassles
G. Big Brother and the Holding Company
H. The Jim Kweskin Jug Band
I. The Herd
J. The Great Society
K. The Spencer Davis Group
L. Kilburn and the High Roads
M. The Nazz
N. Wind in the Willows
O. Chicken Shack
P. Zoot
Q. The First Edition
R. Steampacket
S. Bluesology
T. Them

See page 130 for answers.

63

THE IVY LEAGUE ROCK AND ROLL QUIZ BOOK

BETWEEN THE LINES

What song does this line come from? Who performed it?

A. "You don't need a weatherman to know which way the wind blows."
B. "There's a feeling I get when I look to the West."
C. "Meet the new boss, same as the old boss."
D. "She's got electric boots, a mohair suit, you know I read it in a magazine."
E. "Girls will be boys and boys will be girls."
F. "I shouted out, 'Who killed the Kennedys,' when after all it was you and me."
G. "You go strolling through the crowd like Peter Lorre contemplating a crime."
H. "Now they know how many holes it takes to fill the Albert Hall."
I. "Ride the snake to the ancient lake."

THE IVY LEAGUE ROCK AND ROLL QUIZ BOOK

BETWEEN THE LINES

J. "Girls comb their hair in rear-view mirrors and the boys try to look so hard."

K. "One pill makes you larger, and one pill makes you small."

L. " 'Scuse me while I kiss the sky."

M. "Just because a record has a groove don't make it in the groove."

N. "I'm getting bugged driving up and down the same old strip."

O. "Still, a man hears what he wants to hear and disregards the rest."

P. "Mountains come out of the sky and they stand there."

Q. "Sometimes it's not so easy to be the teacher's pet."

R. "A wop bop a loo bop a wop bam boom!"

S. "I like smoke and lightning, heavy metal thunder."

See page 132 for answers.

THE IVY LEAGUE ROCK AND ROLL QUIZ BOOK

WHO WROTE THE BOOK OF LOVE

Match the rocker with the book he or she wrote.

1. Bob Dylan
2. Ian Hunter
3. Patti Smith
4. Jim Carroll
5. Jim Morrison
6. Yoko Ono
7. Charlie Watts
8. John Lennon
9. George Harrison
10. Bette Midler

A. *Grapefruit*
B. *In His Own Write*
C. *Seventh Heaven*
D. *Tarantula*
E. *Reflections of a Rock Star*
F. *The Basketball Diaries*
G. *The Lords and New Creatures*
H. *Ode to a High-Flying Bird*
I. *A View From A Broad*
J. *I Me Mine*

What performer was the subject of this rock biography?

11. *No One Here Gets Out Alive*
12. *Buried Alive*
13. *Shout!*
14. *Death of a Rebel*
15. *Born to Run*
16. *Hellfire*
17. *Your Cheatin' Heart*
18. *'Scuze Me While I Kiss the Sky*
19. *No Commercial Potential*
20. *Full Moon*

See page 133 for answers.

THE IVY LEAGUE ROCK AND ROLL QUIZ BOOK

MYSTERY ROCK STAR #8

This retiring and demure young lady appears to be readying herself for some dreaming!

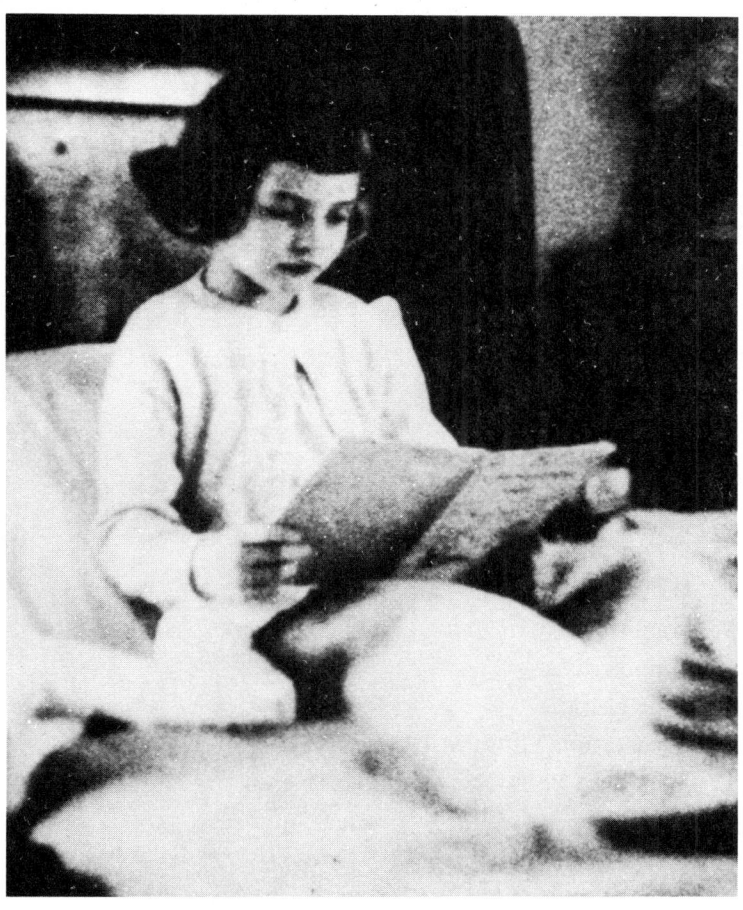

See page 142 for answers.

DIFFERENT DRUM

To what band does—or did—this drummer belong?

1. Keith Moon
2. Gina Schock
3. Maurice White
4. Spencer Dryden
5. Dennis Wilson
6. Max Weinberg
7. Topper Headon
8. John Densmore
9. John Bonham
10. Peter Criss

Who beats on the skins for this band?

11. The Police
12. The Jimi Hendrix Experience
13. The Rolling Stones
14. The Kinks
15. The Band
16. Creedence Clearwater Revival
17. The Monkees
18. The Talking Heads
19. The Beatles
20. Cheap Trick

See page 134 for answers.

THE IVY LEAGUE ROCK AND ROLL QUIZ BOOK

NO BASSIST IN FACT

Here's the bassist—what band does (or did) he play with?

1. John Entwistle
2. Pete Farndon
3. Berry Oakley
4. Tina Weymouth
5. Sid Vicious
6. Roger Waters
7. John Bentley
8. Sting
9. Peter Cetera
10. Chas Chandler

To rephrase things—name the bass player for this band.

11. Led Zeppelin
12. The E Street Band
13. The Clash
14. Creedence Clearwater Revival
15. The Rolling Stones
16. The Go-Gos
17. Fleetwood Mac
18. Yes
19. The Grateful Dead
20. KISS

See page 135 for answers.

ROCK LOCKS

Identify the rock and roll stars by these disembodied hairstyles.

1.

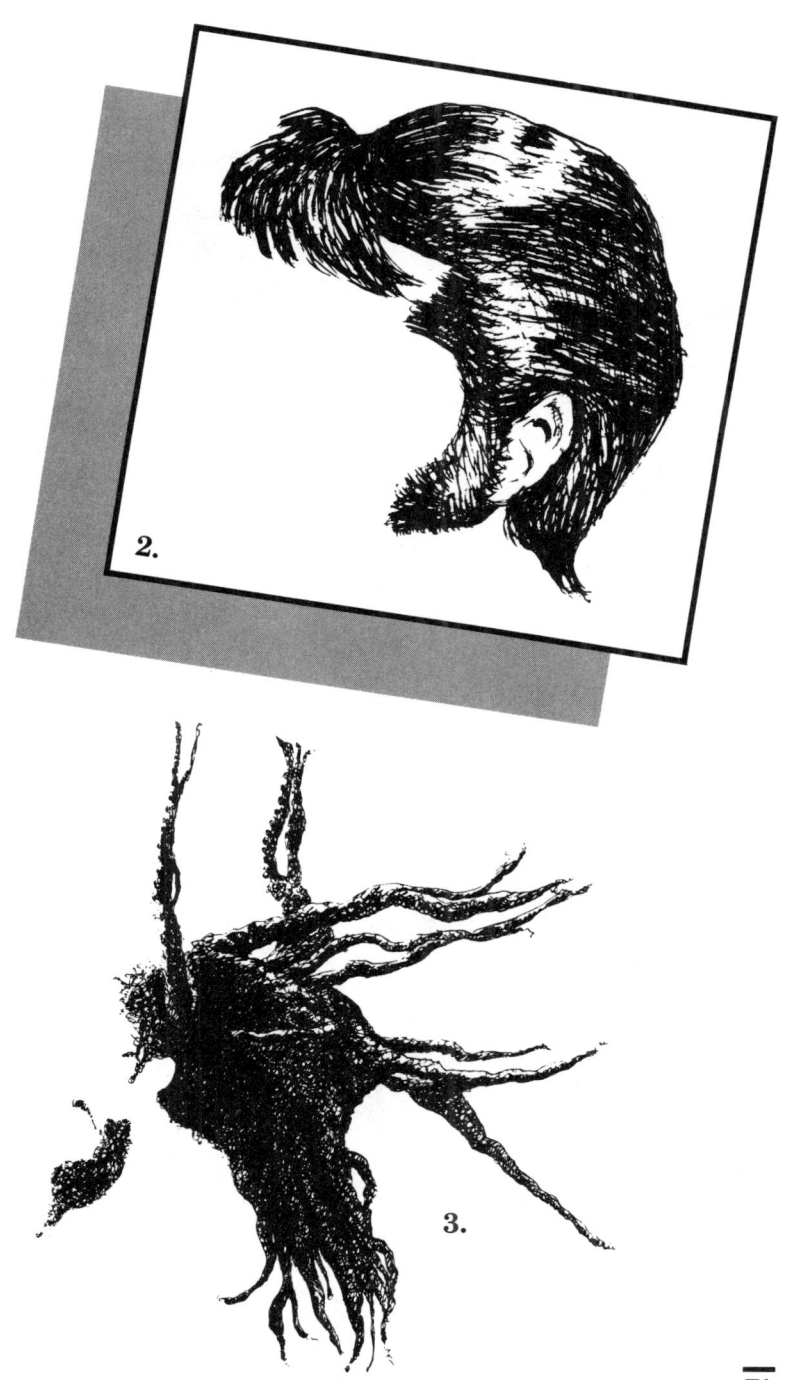

ROCK LOCKS

4.

5.

6.

7.

ROCK LOCKS

8.

See page 135 for answers.

9.

10.

THE IVY LEAGUE ROCK AND ROLL QUIZ BOOK

MYSTERY ROCK STAR #9

When the grass was greener and the world was brand-new to this future member of one of history's greatest rock band.

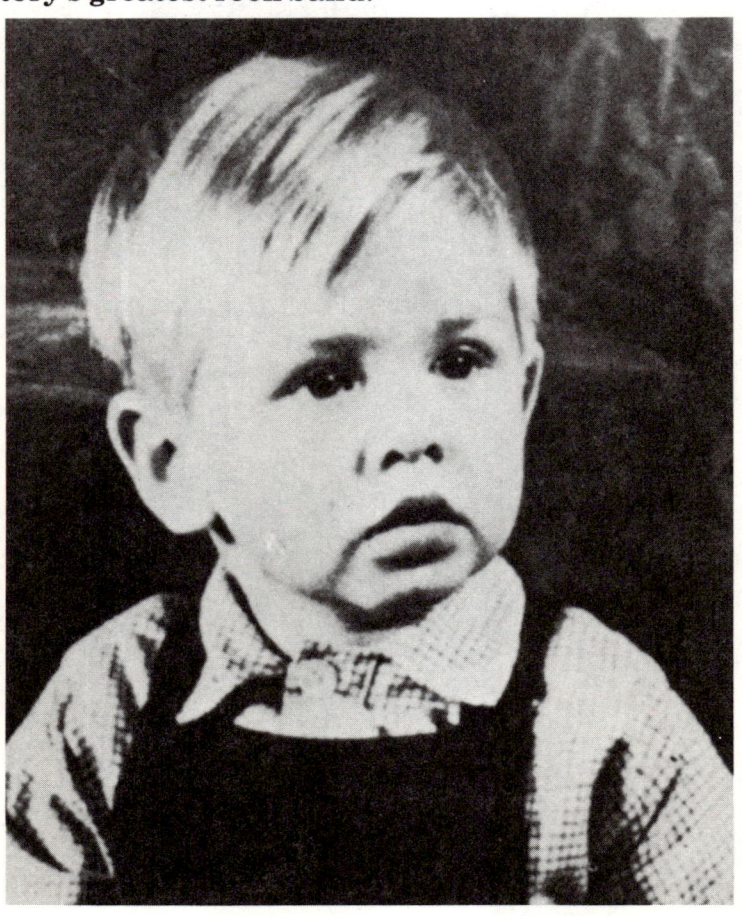

See page 142 for answers.

THE IVY LEAGUE ROCK AND ROLL QUIZ BOOK
JUKE BOX HEROES

For which band does this person play lead guitar?

1. Pete Townshend
2. Ann Wilson
3. Mark Farner
4. Alex Lifeson
5. Jerry Garcia
6. Billy Gibbons
7. Nile Rodgers
8. Keith Richards
9. Martin Barre
10. Paul Weller

Who plays lead guitar for this band?

11. Queen
12. The Police
13. The Doors
14. The Pretenders
15. Cheap Trick
16. The Band
17. Mahogany Rush
18. Dire Straits
19. The Kinks
20. Blue Oyster Cult

See page 136 for answers.

CRY OF LOVE

Many bands and performers have special rallying cries, slogans identified with them that they might utter in concert or that fans might chant. Whose rallying cries are these?

1. "It's too late to stop now!"
2. "On your feet or on your knees!"
3. "Hey! Ho! Let's go!"
4. "Uncle Jam wants you!"
5. "Get yer ya-yas out!"
6. "Dance to the music!"
7. "Kick out the jams, motherfuckers!"
8. "Are we not men?"
9. "The South's gonna do it again!"
10. "Got my mojo working!"

See page 137 for answers.

THE IVY LEAGUE ROCK AND ROLL QUIZ BOOK

LOVE THAT DIRTY WATER

Supply the missing word in each water-related song title.

1. "Who'll Stop the _____," Creedence Clearwater Revival
2. "Black _____," The Doobie Brothers
3. "Down By the _____," Neil Young
4. "Up On Cripple _____," The Band
5. "Fire _____,"Bob Seger
6. "_____ Cruise,"Frankie Ford
7. "_____ City," Jan and Dean
8. "Down in the _____," Bob Dylan
9. "Catch A _____," The Beach Boys
10. "The Tracks of My _____," Smokey Robinson and the Miracles

See page 137 for answers.

THE IVY LEAGUE ROCK AND ROLL QUIZ BOOK

MYSTERY ROCK STAR #10

Obviously an avid reader even at this young age, the babe with the book will be reading all about himself one day!

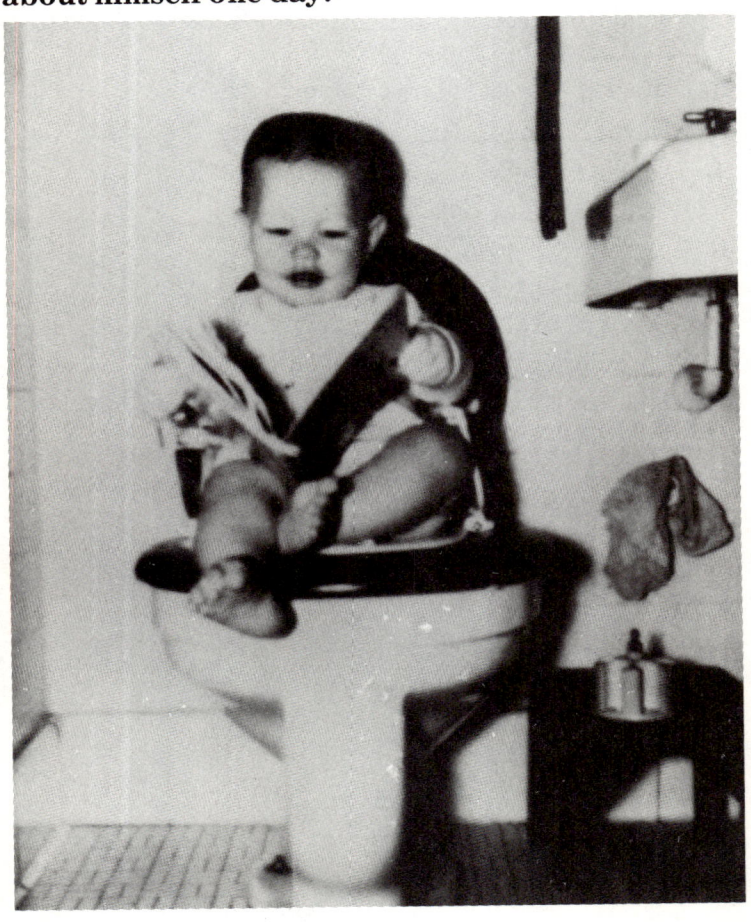

See page 142 for answers.

80

THE IVY LEAGUE ROCK AND ROLL QUIZ BOOK

DANCING IN THE STREET

Match the dance craze and the person or group that began it.

1. "Mashed Potato Time"   A. Rufus Thomas
2. "The Twist"   B. Dion
3. "The Hustle"   C. Little Eva
4. "Le Freak"   D. Chic
5. "The Majestic"   E. Chubby Checker
6. "The Popcorn"   F. The Diamonds
7. "The Stroll"   G. Dee Dee Sharp
8. "The Funky Chicken"   H. James Brown
9. "Do The Freddie"   I. Van McCoy
10. "The Loco-Motion"   J. Freddy and the Dreamers

EXTRA CREDIT: *Which rock star invented the Pogo, the quintessential Punk dance step, because he couldn't dance?*

See page 138 for answers.

81

THE IVY LEAGUE ROCK AND ROLL QUIZ BOOK

SPEAKING WORDS OF WISDOM

Who said it?

1. "When you get in the record business, someone gonna rip you anyway, so that don't bother me. If you don't rip me, she gonna rip me, and if she don't rip me, he gonna rip me, so I'm gonna get ripped. So you don't be bothered by that, because people round you gonna rip you if they can."
    a. *Pat Boone*
    b. *Muddy Waters*
    c. *Little Richard*

2. "I enjoy life. I think I'll enjoy death even more. Life is too confusing."
    a. *David Lee Roth*
    b. *Janis Joplin*
    c. *Cat Stevens*

3. "People take us far too seriously. We're going to have to start being far more stupid."
    a. *David Byrne*
    b. *Frank Zappa*
    c. *Don Kirschner*

4. "I wonder what all the fuss is about. We're the nicest bunch of guys you'd ever want to meet."
    a. *Alice Cooper*
    b. *Keith Richard*
    c. *Johnny Rotten*

5. "I don't take drugs. I've seen great musicians become nothing but snivelling, diseased mon-

THE IVY LEAGUE ROCK AND ROLL QUIZ BOOK
SPEAKING WORDS OF WISDOM

grels because of drugs. It's only a lesser person that takes drugs, and no way am I gonna be that."
- **a.** *Grace Slick*
- **b.** *Donny Osmond*
- **c.** *Ted Nugent*

6. "The only things I was ever in love with were a mirror and a beer mug."
   - **a.** *Sid Vicious*
   - **b.** *Rod Stewart*
   - **c.** *Jerry Lee Lewis*

7. "Rock 'n' roll is phony and false, and sung, written, and played, for the most part, by cretinous goons."
   - **a.** *Frank Sinatra*
   - **b.** *Spiro Agenew*
   - **c.** *Luciano Pavarotti*

8. "I can do anything. One of these days I'll be so complete I won't be human. I'll be a god."
   - **a.** *Jeff Beck*
   - **b.** *Jim Morrison*
   - **c.** *John Denver*

9. "I declare that The Beatles are mutants, prototypes of evolutionary agents endowed with a mysterious power to create a new human species—a young race of laughing freemen."
   - **a.** *Timothy Leary*
   - **b.** *John Lennon*
   - **c.** *David Crosby*

See page 139 for answers.

THE IVY LEAGUE ROCK AND ROLL QUIZ BOOK

HE'S SO FINE

Name the man mentioned in each song.

1. "Leader of the Pack," The Shangri-Las
2. "Ballad of a Thin Man," Bob Dylan
3. "Mrs. Robinson," Simon and Garfunkel
4. "Muskrat Love," The Captain and Tennille
5. "Space Oddity," David Bowie
6. "Do It Again," Steely Dan
7. "Lido Shuffle," Boz Scaggs
8. "Da Doo Ron Ron," The Crystals
9. "Meeting Across the River," Bruce Springsteen
10. "You Can't Always Get What You Want," The Rolling Stones

See page 139 for answers.

FEEL LIKE A NUMBER

Who performed this "number" song?

1. "98.6"
2. "Jenny/867-5309"
3. "One"
4. "I'm Eighteen"
5. "In the Year 2525"
6. "Sixteen Candles"
7. "Twelve Thirty"
8. "25 or 6 to 4"
9. "If 6 Was 9"
10. "Quarter to Three"

See page 140 for answers.

THE IVY LEAGUE ROCK AND ROLL QUIZ BOOK

MYSTERY ROCK STAR #11

He strikes the pose that makes the young girls sigh.

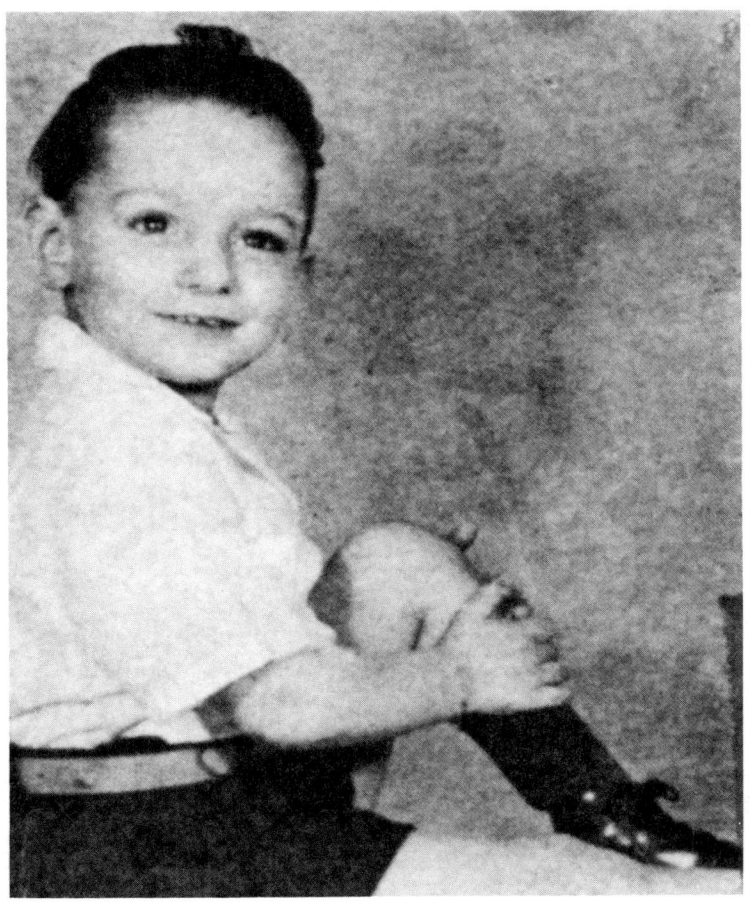

See page 142 for answers.

THE IVY LEAGUE ROCK AND ROLL QUIZ BOOK

GIRLS TALK

Match the girl group and its hit.

1. The Shirelles
2. The Crystals
3. The Chantels
4. The Chiffons
5. The Angels
6. The Shangri-Las
7. The Dixie Cups
8. The Marvelettes
9. The Ad-Libs
10. The Go-Gos
11. The Ronettes
12. Patti LaBelle and the Bluebelles
13. The Supremes
14. The Cookies
15. Martha and the Vandellas

A. "The Boy From New York City"
B. "My Boyfriend's Back"
C. "Maybe"
D. "I Sold My Heart to the Junkman"
E. "He's A Rebel"
F. "Dancing in the Street"
G. "Our Lips Are Sealed"
H. "Leader of the Pack"
I. "Mama Said"
J. "Chains"
K. "Chapel of Love"
L. "You Keep Me Hangin' On"
M. "Be My Baby"
N. "The Hunter Gets Captured By the Game"
O. "He's So Fine"

See page 141 for answers.

THE IVY LEAGUE ROCK QUIZ

Each of these performers attended a college affiliated with the Ivy League. Which one?

1. Tom Scholz
2. Richard Carpenter
3. Bonnie Raitt
4. Art Garfunkel
5. Pete Seeger
6. Laurie Anderson

A. Harvard
B. Radcliffe
C. M.I.T.
D. Columbia
E. Barnard
F. Yale Conservatory of Music

EXTRA CREDIT: *What '70s rock group met at Columbia University?*

See page 141 for answers.

ANSWERS

THE IVY LEAGUE ROCK AND ROLL QUIZ BOOK
ANSWERS

SAME NAME

1. "Stairway to Heaven" (I am <u>not</u> making this up)
2. "Lady"
3. "Shining Star"
4. "The Wanderer"
5. "Tapestry"
6. "Turn Me Loose"
7. "Don't Bring Me Down"
8. "Fame"
9. "Fire"
10. "Woman In Love"
11. "Mother"
12. "Only The Lonely"
13. "Gloria"

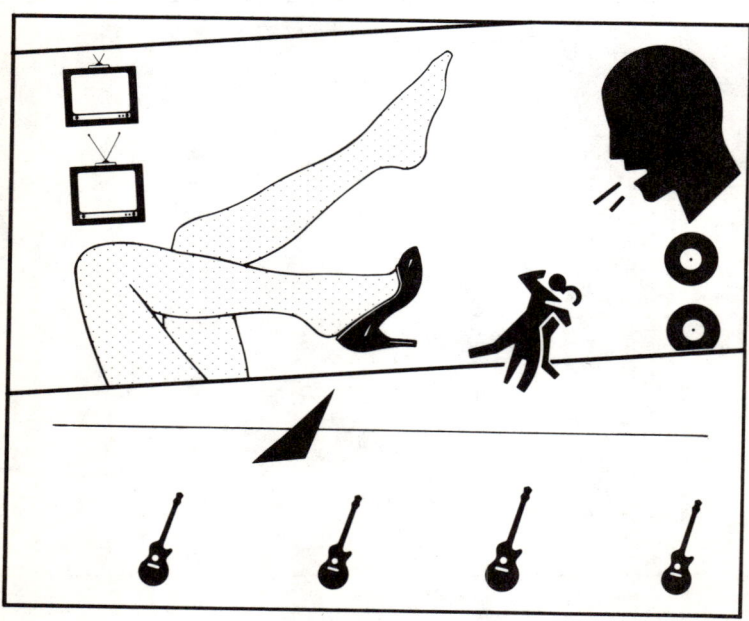

ANSWERS

IDENTITY CRISIS

1. Don McLean, of *American Pie* fame
2. "This is the story of Johnny Rotten"
3. Judy Collins
4. Elton John, *nee* Reginald Dwight
5. Peter Fonda is "She," after an acid trip in which he repeatedly droned, "I know what it's like to be dead." Listen to the song for the rest of the conversation.
6. Warren Beatty
7. Marilyn Monroe
8. Carole King
9. Marianne Faithfull, Mick's '60s girlfriend
10. Graham Nash—"Willie" was her pet name for him when they lived together in the late '60s, early '70s
11. Joni Mitchell, by Graham Nash (turnabout . . .)
12. Bob Dylan
13. Rita Coolidge, by Leon Russell
14. Annette Funicello, by George!
15. Paul McCartney is the subject of this utterly vicious attack
16. Paul McCartney is the author of this utterly guileless paean
17. Queen
18. Elton John
19. George Harrison, with Ringo, Paul, and Linda McCartney

ANSWERS

CAN WE CALL YOU BRUCE?

1. Bruce Springsteen
2. Elvis Presley
3. John Entwistle of The Who (his nickname within the band is "The Mayor of Ealing")
4. Jerry Garcia of The Grateful Dead
5. Chris Squire of Yes
6. James Brown (also known as Soul Brother Number One, Mr. Dynamite, and "The Hardest-Working Man in Show Business!")
7. Jerry Lee Lewis, and you better not forget it
8. Jim Morrison
9. Todd Rundgren
10. Clarence Clemons of the E Street Band
11. Eric Clapton
12. Daryl Dragon
13. Fats Domino
14. James Ulmer, brilliant fusion guitarist
15. Peter Noone of Herman's Hermits
16. David Bowie
17. John Bonham of Led Zeppelin
18. Barry White, uh huh, you know, baby
19. Mick Jagger and Keith Richards (their usual production credit)
20. John Lennon and Paul McCartney (their stage name when performing as a twosome in their Liverpudlian youth)

ANSWERS

SANTA WITHOUT A CLAUSE

1. K
2. G
3. H
4. J
5. N
6. F
7. I
8. E (extra points if you knew their name before the High Numbers—The Detours)
9. C (from when Diana and the girls backed up the Temptations, then known as The Primes)
10. M (would I lie to you? About <u>this</u>?)
11. L
12. D
13. B
14. O
15. A

EXTRA CREDIT: *Jethro Tull. They arrived at the Tull name when, for the first time, they were received well enough to be invited back to a venue. "Jethro Tull" had been their Name of the Week.*

ANSWERS

MR. MOONLIGHT

1. Eric Clapton
2. Joe Walsh
3. Keyboardist Jerry Harrison
4. Drummer Kenney Jones
5. Steve Winwood
6. John Lydon, formerly Johnny Rotten
7. Mick Jones
8. David Crosby—the other members of CSNY came from The Hollies (Nash) and Buffalo Springfield (Stills, Young)
9. Singer Paul Rodgers
10. Randy Bachman
11. Ron Wood
12. Bob Weir (later to launch Bobby and the Midnites as well)
13. Rod Argent
14. David Freiberg, guitar hero
15. Denny Laine, guitar stalwart
16. Carl Palmer, originally of Atomic Rooster (well, it was the 60's)
17. Leslie West, a mountain in his own right
18. Eric Burdon, too black for the former and too white for the latter
19. Miami Steve Van Zandt
20. Keith Emerson

THE IVY LEAGUE ROCK AND ROLL QUIZ BOOK

ANSWERS

STORMY WEATHER

1. Rain
2. Wind
3. Hurricane
4. Breeze
5. Storm
6. Lightnin'
7. Snow
8. Cloud
9. Sun
10. Shower (sorry 'bout that . . .)

WILL THE REAL BALDEMAR HUERTA PLEASE STAND UP?

A. 8
B. 9
C. 1
D. 3 (the real Baldemar Huerta!)
E. 2
F. 12
G. 7
H. 5
I. 4
J. 11
K. 6
L. 13
M. 10

ANSWERS

HELLO, IT'S ME

1. *Freak Out!*
2. *Cold Spring Harbor.* Joel's first album was mastered at the wrong speed, leading some to speculate that Alvin of the Chipmunks had finally released a solo album.
3. *My Aim Is True*
4. *This Was*
5. *Greetings From Asbury Park, N.J.*, which failed commercially after an attempt to promote Springsteen as "the new Bob Dylan" backfired.
6. *The Grateful Dead*
7. *Outlandos D'Amour.* They didn't *really* make an album called *Magilla Gorilla*.
8. *Meet the Beatles!* was their first American release; *The Beatles* is the official name of the record universally called "The White Album"; it was actually the Rolling Stones' first album that was credited to "England's Newest Hitmakers"; and *We're Gonna Change the Face of Pop Music Forever* is the name of the Beatles' first album in Mark Shipper's satirical Beatle fantasy, *Paperback Writer.*
9. *Are You Experienced?*
10. *Wednesday Morning, 3 A.M.*, featuring the original acoustic version of "The Sounds of Silence."

ANSWERS

I WRITE THE SONGS

1. Neil Diamond, who also wrote the Monkees hit "A Little Bit Me, A Little Bit You"
2. Joni Mitchell
3. Leon Russell
4. Bobby Womack, soul singer
5. Paul Anka, who also dashed off the theme song for "The Tonight Show"
6. Gene Pitney, author of "He's A Rebel" for The Crystals
7. Cat Stevens
8. Bruce Springsteen
9. Bob Dylan
10. Neil Sedaka
11. David Bowie, who also produced the song
12. Carole King
13. Randy Newman. He lived off the royalties for years.
14. Neil Young
15. Laura Nyro

ANSWERS

YOU CAN ALL JOIN IN

1. Eric Clapton, who also plays on the second side of *Abbey Road*
2. David Bowie, who produced the song
3. Jimmy Page of Led Zeppelin, formerly a session pro who can also be heard on "I Can't Explain" by the Who and "Gloria" by Them.
4. Junior Walker, minus the Allstars
5. Flo (the Phlorescent Leech) and Eddie, formerly of the Turtles and The Mothers of Invention
6. Nicky Hopkins, who seemed to play on every record of the late '60s
7. Phil Spector
8. Carole King, who was dissatisfied with the drummer hired to lay on this, the first big hit she wrote
9. Mick Jagger
10. Billy Preston
11. George Harrison, who co-wrote the track
12. Marvin Gaye
13. Elton John
14. Duane Allman
15. Elvis Costello

MASS PRODUCTION

1. *D.* This album was a by-product of Lennon's year-

ANSWERS

long "Lost Weekend" in L.A. following his separation from Yoko Ono. In between binges with Nilsson, Ringo, and Keith Moon, John squeezed out this chaotic album—his only credited production job.

2. *F.* Thunderclap Newman, whose only album this was, consisted of Townshend crony and keyboard whiz Andy Newman, ex-Who roadie Speedy Keen, and future Wings guitarist Jimmy McCullough (17 years old at the time).

3. *H.* Rundgren, whose studio expertise is legendary, has also produced Meat Loaf.

4. *J.* Doors keyboardist Manzarek has produced all of X's albums.

5. *A.* Lowe learned his craft from fellow Rockpiler Dave Edmunds.

6. *E.* Bowie also produced Mott the Hoople.

7. *B.* Petty's attempt to rejuvenate Shannon followed closely Bruce Springsteen's similar service for Shannon contemporary Gary "U.S." Bonds. Petty was not quite as successful.

8. *G.* It is this connection that accounts for Diamond's uncomfortable presence at The Band's "Last Waltz," the mammoth concert/film in which Robertson's group bid farewell to performing.

9. *I.* Squeeze vocalist Glenn Tilbrook returned the favor by dueting with Elvis on the Costello album *Trust*.

10. *C.* The head Bee Gee had a hand in Streisand smashes like "A Woman In Love" and the title track.

THE IVY LEAGUE ROCK AND ROLL QUIZ BOOK
ANSWERS

ALL BY MYSELF

1. Ron Wood
2. Joe Walsh
3. John Entwistle
4. Ozzy Osbourne
5. Jon Anderson
6. George Harrison
7. Phil Collins
8. Grace Slick
9. Boz Scaggs (really!)
10. Rod Stewart
11. Lou Reed
12. Brian Eno
13. David Byrne—his score for Twyla Tharp's ballet
14. Steve Winwood

HOT SPACES

1. (They Long to Be)
2. (Naturally)
3. (I Know)
4. (The Way I Love You)
5. (I Can't Get No)
6. (I Feel Good)
7. (Jammin')
8. (The Angels Wanna Wear My)
9. (This Bird Has Flown)
10. (And I'll Cry If I Want To)
11. (Your Love Keeps Lifting Me)
12. (I'm Only Bleeding)
13. (In a Field of Stone)
14. (Wish I Could Fly Like)
15. (Rock Me A Little While)

ANSWERS

SHE'S A WOMAN

1. Judy
2. Marie
3. Emily
4. Jane
5. Sally
6. Sherry
7. Sara
8. Leyna
9. Rikki
10. Rhonda

MEANINGLESS BUT TRUE

1. The Crystals, featuring (on this song only) Cher, who didn't make it big for another two years
2. Little Anthony and the Imperials
3. Manfred Mann, who also hit with "Sha La La"
4. The Police
5. The Coasters—another great teenage cartoon written by Jerry Lieber and Mike Stoller (others include "Charlie Brown," "Jailhouse Rock," and Elvis knows how many more)
6. The Iron Butterfly. The title was supposed to mean "In the garden of Eden," or something like that
7. Gene Vincent and the Blue Caps
8. Lee Dorsey, originator of "Working in a Coal Mine"
9. The Beatles, Paul in particular
10. A Taste of Honey

ANSWERS

I GOT A WOMAN

1. Wendy
2. Virginia
3. Kathy
4. Mary
5. Susie
6. Susan
7. Mother Mary
8. Sleepy Jean
9. Rita
10. Sally

UNDER THE COVERS

A. "The Loco-motion"
B. "Oh Pretty Woman"
C. "Crimson and Clover"
D. "Wonderful World" (Garfunkel's version has James Taylor and Paul Simon on backup vocals)
E. "The Lion Sleeps Tonight" (based on the Weavers' hit "Wimoweh," in turn based on an African folk-song)
F. "(Your Love Keeps Lifting Me) Higher and Higher"
G. "You're Sixteen" (written by the Sherman brothers, later to pen—*Mary Poppins*?)
H. "Roll Over, Beethoven"
I. "Da Doo Ron Ron" (the then-unknown Cher sings on the original)

THE IVY LEAGUE ROCK AND ROLL QUIZ BOOK

ANSWERS

- **J.** "You've Lost That Loving Feeling"
- **K.** "Never Can Say Goodbye"
- **L.** "MacArthur Park"
- **M.** "Soul Man" (a note-for-note copy played with members of the original Memphis band)
- **N.** Merilee Rush
- **O.** Buddy Holly
- **P.** Bruce Springsteen (Manfred Mann's version is drastically different)
- **Q.** Frankie Lymon and the Teenagers
- **R.** Maurice Williams and the Zodiacs
- **S.** Bob Marley and the Wailers
- **T.** Roy Orbison
- **U.** Al Green
- **V.** The Band
- **W.** Jimmy Jones
- **X.** The Chiffons (King co-wrote the song with then-husband Gerry Goffin)
- **Y.** B.J. Thomas (the strangest transformation of the bunch—Blue Swede's version is backed by the chant, "Ooga-chucka, ooga-chucka, ooga-ooga-ooga-chucka!")
- **Z.** Cannibal and the Headhunters

THE IVY LEAGUE ROCK AND ROLL QUIZ BOOK

ANSWERS

THE MAN IN THE GLASS BOOTH

1. *G.* (Martin's other productions include almost every Beatles record, America, and Cheap Trick)
2. *D.* (Spector you should know)
3. *H.* (Perry's other slick, seamless albums include *Ringo* and Barbra Streisand's *Stoney End*)
4. *E.* (Baker also produces Queen)
5. *J.* (Miller produced for Traffic as well as helming such classic Stones albums as *Let It Bleed*)
6. *A.* (Johns has also worked with The Eagles and The Clash)
7. *C.* (Johnston, inactive for years, can look back with satisfaction on Dylan's *Highway 61 Revisited* and *Johnny Cash at Folsom Prison*)
8. *I.* (Ramone, whose live production expertise can be heard on Joel's *Songs in the Attic* LP, is credited by many with transforming the careers of Joel and Paul Simon)
9. *F.* (How much of this classic album Warhol actually produced is a matter of conjecture—it is certainly his only credit)
10. *B.* (That's right, the same man who heads the Alan Parsons Project, for which he neither sings nor plays)

THE IVY LEAGUE ROCK AND ROLL QUIZ BOOK

ANSWERS

ONE PILL MAKES YOU LARGER

1. B
2. A
3. C
4. A
5. C
6. A
7. B
8. C
9. A
10. C

TAKING CARE OF BUSINESS

1. I
2. H
3. E
4. C
5. B
6. J
7. F
8. D
9. G
10. A

ANSWERS

WORDS OF LOVE

1. Carl Perkins (The Fab Four also covered his "Honey Don't" and "Everybody Wants to Be My Baby")
2. Chuck Berry, natch
3. Buddy Holly
4. Barrett Strong, an early Motown great
5. Buck Owens (chalk it up to Ringo's love of country music—before making it as a drummer, he wrote to the state of Texas inquiring about employment as a cowboy)
6. Larry Williams (the nearly forgotten Williams also wrote "Bad Boy" and "Slow Down," both of which got the Beatle treatment)
7. Little Richard (Pauls' screaming imitation of Richard was the traditional close of nearly every Beatles concert from the Hamburg days on)
8. The Isley Brothers
9. The Shirelles
10. The Marvelettes

ANSWERS

GET IT RIGHT THE FIRST TIME

1. "Proud Mary"
2. "Rainy Day Women 12 and 35"
3. "Baba O'Riley"
4. "The 59th Street Bridge Song"
5. "Hey Hey, My My (Into the Black)"
6. "White Rabbit"
7. "For What It's Worth"
8. "Little T & A"
9. "Space Oddity"
10. "Weekend In New England"

THE IVY LEAGUE ROCK AND ROLL QUIZ BOOK
ANSWERS

WE GOTTA GET OUT OF THIS PLACE

A. 6
B. 10
C. 5
D. 12 (honestly!)
E. 3
F. 8
G. 2
H. 4
I. 11
J. 9
K. 1
L. 7
M. 18 (on a fencing scholarship)
N. 16
O. 14 (Sarah Lawrence was also home to Lesley Gore, Linda McCartney, and Yoko Ono)
P. 13
Q. 19
R. 17
S. 15
T. 20

BODY LANGUAGE

1. Eyes
2. Lips
3. Heart
4. Shoulder
5. Fingertips
6. Legs
7. Thumb
8. Hand
9. Face
10. Head

ANSWERS

GET TOGETHER

1. "Under Pressure"
2. "No More Tears (Enough Is Enough)"
3. "Don't Go Breaking My Heart"
4. "Gone At Last"
5. "Ebony and Ivory" (extra credit if you said "What's That You're Doing," which wasn't a single)
6. "Take Off"
7. "You Don't Bring Me Flowers"
8. "Fame" (the song is credited only to Bowie, but Lennon co-wrote it and sings every other line)
9. "Gimme Shelter" (whatever happened to Merry Clayton?)
10. "All Those Years Ago"

EXTRA CREDIT:

A. "All You Need Is Love," The Beatles. *Mick Jagger sings a bar of "She Loves You" at the fade-out.*
B. "We Love You," The Rolling Stones. *John Lennon and Paul McCartney sing on this single, released after Mick and Keith Richards were released from jail (drug charges, of course).*

ANSWERS

LEADER OF THE PACK

1. The Yardbirds (Relf co-founded Renaissance as well, but yielded the lead vocalist spot to Annie Haslam)
2. Steppenwolf
3. Manfred Mann (Mann himself was the keyboardist). Bruce Springsteen has called Jones his favorite singer
4. Yes
5. Lynyrd Skynyrd
6. Thin Lizzy
7. Foreigner
8. Blue Oyster Cult
9. The Clash
10. Rush
11. The Rolling Stones, according to *Who's Who*
12. REO Speedwagon
13. The Talking Heads
14. The Doors
15. The Guess Who

ANSWERS

PACK OF THE LEADER

1. Chrissie Hynde
2. Robin Zander, who isn't *really* as much of a twit as he sounds on *Live at Budokan*
3. John Fogerty, who also wrote and produced CCR's astonishing string of hits
4. Sting
5. Ray Davies
6. Peter Wolf (J. Geils is the lead guitarist)
7. Roger Daltry
8. The unique (fortunately) David Lee Roth, insured by Lloyd's of London against paternity suits
9. Brad Delp
10. Peter Noone, the single greatest influence on the vocals of the punk band The Ramones
11. Robert Plant
12. John Sebastian
13. Janis Joplin
14. Steve Marriott, formerly of the Small Faces
15. Paul Rodgers

THE IVY LEAGUE ROCK AND ROLL QUIZ BOOK

ANSWERS

MY LITTLE TOWN

1. Detroit (also home to Mitch Ryder and the Detroit Wheels and Grand Funk Railroad—a rock and roll town all the way)
2. Boston (hmmm . . . nice name for a group . . .)
3. San Francisco (from whence Santana, The Grateful Dead, Country Joe and the Fish, and countless other all-time great bands came)
4. New York, New York (that helluva town)
5. Los Angeles (the world renowned Capital of Mellow—just ask Black Flag, X, The Knack, Frank Zappa . . .)
6. New Orleans (son of a gun, we'll have good fun on the bayou)
7. Memphis, Tennessee (as the song goes)
8. The sound of Philadelphia
9. Chicago (another great name for a group, don't you think?
10. London town

LONDON CALLING

1. C
2. C
3. B
4. A
5. A
6. A
7. C
8. B
9. C
10. C

THE IVY LEAGUE ROCK AND ROLL QUIZ BOOK

ANSWERS

WITH A LITTLE HELP FROM MY FRIENDS

1. Elvis Costello
2. Frankie Valli, whose falsetto reportedly can shatter plastic
3. Buddy Holly. Waylon Jennings was once a Cricket
4. Tom Petty
5. James Brown
6. Bruce Springsteen
7. Frankie Lymon, of "Why Do Fools Fall in Love" fame
8. Tommy James, who thinks we're alone now
9. Bette Midler
10. Bob Marley
11. The Blackhearts
12. The Shadows, who racked up a sizable number of hits on their own
13. The Dakotas
14. The Chartbusters
15. The Tennessee Three, often featuring Carl Perkins
16. The Silver Bullet Band
17. The Detroit Wheels (extra credit if you mentioned Detroit, Ryder's second band)
18. The Miracles
19. The News
20. The Modern Lovers

ANSWERS

A NIGHT AT THE OPERA

1. The Pretty Things. This was the very first rock opera, unless you count *The Who Sell Out,* which is unified by a concept but not by storyline.
2. The Who. Of course. The only rock opera on this list to have been performed at the Metropolitan Opera House.
3. Pink Floyd
4. Lou Reed
5. Frank Zappa
6. The Kinks
7. The Bonzo Dog Doo Dah Band
8. Cat Stevens
9. Randy Newman
10. Jethro Tull

TWO FOR THE SHOW

1. Double
2. Double
3. Single
4. Double
5. Single
6. Triple
7. Double
8. Single
9. Single
10. Double

ANSWERS

FREEZE-FRAME

1. Ringo Starr
2. The Dave Clark Five—who, strangely, do not sing or play on camera in this film by John Boorman (he went on to do *Deliverance* and *Excalibur*, to name two)
3. Neil Young
4. Led Zeppelin
5. Frank Zappa (also features Ringo Starr and Flo & Eddie)
6. Elvis Presley, as a doctor who tempts nun Mary Tyler Moore to cast off her whimple
7. David Bowie, who astonished critics and fans with his fine performance
8. The Sex Pistols and their manager, the outrageous Malcolm McLaren
9. The Clash
10. Bob Dylan—his excruciating home movies of the 1976 Rolling Thunder Revue

THE IVY LEAGUE ROCK AND ROLL QUIZ BOOK
ANSWERS

11. Paul Simon, who also wrote the screenplay
12. Deborah Harry of Blondie, with brown hair
13. The Rolling Stones, with particular emphasis on Mick
14. The Rutles—a loving Beatles parody with an appearance by George
15. Reggae sensation Jimmy Cliff
16. James Taylor (Dennis Wilson also attempts to act here)
17. The Ramones
18. Roy Orbison
19. Bette Midler, doing a thinly disguised Janis Joplin
20. The Monkees, with a cameo appearance by Frank Zappa. The stars appear in one sequence as dandruff in the hair of Victor Mature.

ANSWERS

CELLULOID HEROES

A. *The Spy Who Loved Me* (the 11th James Bond film)
B. *Thank God It's Friday*
C. *Saturday Night Fever*
D. *Butch Cassidy and the Sundance Kid*
E. *One-Trick Pony,* written and starred in by Simon
F. *Rocky III*
G. *Pat Garrett and Billy the Kid* (in which Dylan plays "Alias")
H. *American Gigolo*
I. *The Graduate*
J. *A Star is Born* (Streisand also wrote the music)
K. Paul McCartney and Wings
L. Diana Ross and Lionel Richie
M. Barbra Streisand
N. Frankie Valli (minus the 4 Seasons: song written by Barry Gibb)
O. Curtis Mayfield
P. Dolly Parton
Q. Vangelis
R. David Gates (without Bread)
S. Earth, Wind, & Fire
T. Jerry Lee Lewis (his last hit before being blacklisted for marrying his 13-year-old cousin Myra Gale)

ANSWERS

SLEEPING WITH THE TELEVISION ON

1. F
2. D
3. A
4. H
5. E

6. I
7. C
8. B
9. G
10. J

IT'S ALIVE!

1. Lou Reed
2. The MC 5 (It stood for Motor City, i.e. Detroit)
3. The Who
4. The Band
5. Emerson, Lake, and Palmer
6. Jethro Tull
7. The Rolling Stones (their *yawn* fourth live set)
8. Neil Young
9. The Doors
10. Jefferson Airplane
11. Blue Oyster Cult
12. Deep Purple
13. Joni Mitchell
14. The Kinks
15. Warren Zevon

ANSWERS

ROCKER MORTIS

1. Allman died in a motorcycle crash, as would his Allman Brothers Band colleague Berry Oakley
2. An automobile accident during which he suffered a fatal heart attack.
3. Ace, riding high on his hit "Pledging My Love," was playing Russian Roulette backstage at a gig. He lost.
4. Cooke was shot by motel manager Bertha Franklin, who claimed he was assaulting her
5. The first leader of the Rolling Stones drowned in his own swimming pool, with a little help from a lot of drugs
6. Holly was killed in a plane crash, along with The Big Bopper and Richie Valens, who had flipped a coin with Waylon Jennings for a seat on the plane
7. Hathaway fell to his death from a high window
8. Heroin overdose
9. Mama Cass choked to death (Keith Moon would die in the same apartment four years later)
10. Heart attack

ANSWERS

SELLING OUT

1. *F* "Wish they all could be Herbal Essence girls..."
2. *K* ("I love I love I love my calendar cat...")
3. *C* ("Whole lotta Shakey's goin' on...")
4. *M* ("Come on, Buick, light my fire...")
5. *B* (They didn't have to change anything)
6. *H* ("I'm soaking up good vibrations, Sunkist is a taste sensation...")
7. *I*
8. *J* ("The M&Ms man...")
9. *L* ("Let's do the Brim twist...")
10. *N* ("If you dare wear shorts shorts, Nair for short shorts...")
11. *D* ("Yummy yummy yummy, got Esskay in my tummy...")
12. *E* ("Up, up, and away, TWA...")
13. G
14. *A* ("You're still having fun, and we're still the one")

EXTRA CREDIT: *"I'd Like to Teach the World to Sing,"* which started life as *"I'd Like to Buy the World a Coke."*

THE IVY LEAGUE ROCK AND ROLL QUIZ BOOK
ANSWERS

YOU'RE ENTITLED

1. Mister
2. Queen
3. King
4. Duke
5. Count (sorry . . .)
6. Mrs.
7. Miss
8. Doctor
9. Private
10. Captain

I CALL YOUR NAME

1. Alice Cooper (real name Vincent Furnier) is the lead singer
2. Jethro Tull invented the seed drill over a century before any of the band members were born
3. Uriah Heep is a character in *David Copperfield* by Charles Dickens
4. Manfred Mann is the keyboardist
5. J. Geils is the lead guitarist
6. God knows who Marshall Tucker is—he isn't in the band
7. No one by that name here
8. Named after a particularly hated gym teacher
9. Named for prurient interest, although the band might deny it
10. Eddie and Alex Van Halen play lead guitar and drums, respectively

THE IVY LEAGUE ROCK AND ROLL QUIZ BOOK
ANSWERS

ON THE ROAD

1. Street (the inspiration, of course, for Bruce Springsteen's "Racing in the Street" and The Rolling Stones' "Street Fighting Man")
2. Alley
3. Road
4. Lane
5. Court
6. Avenue
7. Highway
8. Boardwalk
9. Broadway
10. Row

ANSWERS

I LOVE ROCK AND ROLL

1. The Who
2. Chuck Berry (hit covers by The Beatles and The Beach Boys)
3. Billy Joel
4. Joan Jett and the Blackhearts
5. The Showmen
6. Bob Seger
7. Danny and the Juniors ("At The Hop" was their other hit)
8. Bill Haley and the Comets, of course
9. The Lovin' Spoonful, 'cause the magic's in the music, and the music's in me.
10. Mott the Hoople

THE IVY LEAGUE ROCK AND ROLL QUIZ BOOK

ANSWERS

OFF THE RECORD

1. The jacket is entirely blank except for the words "THE BEATLES" in raised white lettering
2. The album is packaged in a plain brown wrapper
3. The jacket is round
4. The album comes in a cardboard box
5. Figures of the band members "stood up" when you opened the gatefold, like a Pop-Up book
6. The top of the album was attached to the lower jaw and eyes of the man on the cover, so that they bobbed up and down when you pressed the top
7. You could actually peel the banana on the cover, designed by Andy Warhol
8. Warhol was also responsible for this cover, the crotch of a man's trousers featuring a working zipper
9. The Stones' rip-off of/homage to *Sgt. Pepper* had a sleeve in simulated 3-D
10. The title was printed in Braille (or misprinted—Stevie eagerly felt one early copy, only to find that the bumps spelled out "Picture Book")

THE IVY LEAGUE ROCK AND ROLL QUIZ BOOK
ANSWERS

ONE-HIT WONDERS

- **A.** Carl Douglas
- **B.** The Lemon Pipers
- **C.** The Strawberry Alarm Clock
- **D.** The Hollywood Argyles
- **E.** Lipps, Inc.
- **F.** M (which stands for Munich)
- **G.** John Fred and his Playboy Band
- **H.** The Iron Butterfly
- **I.** Thunderclap Newman (produced by Pete Townshend)
- **J.** Rickie Lee Jones (I <u>know</u> she's still around, but this was her only Top 40 hit)
- **K.** Tim Curry (of *The Rocky Horror Picture Show*)
- **L.** David Soul (of *Starsky & Hutch*, no less)
- **M.** Rick Dees and his Cast of Idiots
- **N.** Bobby "Boris" Pickett and the Crypt-Kicker Five

ANSWERS

- **O.** Zager and Evans
- **P.** The Del-Vikings
- **Q.** Barry McGuire (this is the song that kept "Like A Rolling Stone" from hitting #1)
- **R.** The Starland Vocal Band
- **S.** Count Five
- **T.** Debby Boone
- **U.** The Stampeders (they had other hits in Canada, for the meticulous)
- **V.** Thin Lizzy
- **W.** The Youngbloods (led by Jesse Colin Young)
- **X.** Wild Cherry
- **Y.** The Music Machine
- **Z.** Wayne Fontana and the Mindbenders (the Mindbenders minus Fontana had a hit in 1967, "A Groovy Kind of Love")

ANSWERS

I FOUGHT THE LAW

1. *D* (Berry's first tragic conviction was little more than a frame-up)
2. *H* (Berry's second tragic conviction, unfortunately, was not)
3. *J*
4. *A*
5. *G* (Japanese customs authorities arrested Paul at the airport, leading to the cancellation of his Japanese tour)
6. *C*
7. *E* (Vicious died of a heroin OD while awaiting trial for the murder of girlfriend Nancy Spungen)
8. *B* (The Glimmer Twins released their sardonic "We Love You" upon their release)
9. *F*
10. *I* (John, who had the original hit with "Fever" when Peggy Lee was still in bobby sox, died of pneumonia in prison)

THE IVY LEAGUE ROCK AND ROLL QUIZ BOOK
ANSWERS

COMBAT ROCK

1. E (Combat Rock, by the way, is the Clash's 5th album.)
2. B
3. H
4. F
5. D
6. J
7. A
8. I
9. G
10. C

ROCKIN' ALL OVER THE WORLD

1. Australia
2. Sweden. ABBA currently ranks as that country's most profitable industry.
3. Germany (West, of course—punk rocker Nina Hagen is almost certainly the only star to come out of East Germany.)
4. Japan
5. Akron, Ohio
6. Canada
7. The Netherlands, also home to Stars On 45
8. Jamaica, funky Kingston to be specific
9. Ireland
10. England

THE IVY LEAGUE ROCK AND ROLL QUIZ BOOK
ANSWERS

POINT OF ORDER

1. *Meet the Beatles!*
2. *The Beatles' Second Album* (You were expecting maybe *Beatles VI?*)
3. *Something Old Something New*
4. *The Beatles Story*
5. *A Hard Day's Night*
6. *Beatles '65*
7. *Help!*
8. *Rubber Soul*
9. *"Yesterday"... and Today*
10. *Revolver*
11. *Sgt. Pepper's Lonely Hearts Club Band*
12. *Magical Mystery Tour*
13. *The Beatles* (also known as "White Album")
14. *Yellow Submarine*
15. *Abbey Road*
16. *Let It Be*
17. *Hey Jude*

WHERE I'M COMING FROM

1. *E.* The mammoth Dr. Zoom included on-stage Monopoly players.

ANSWERS

2. *P.* Zoot was a top heavy-metal band in Springfield's native Australia.
3. *L*
4. *M*
5. *F*
6. *N.* Harry tried to hide her membership in the hippie-era Wind in the Willows after Blondie took off—it wasn't cool, and it indicated correctly that she is older than she looks.
7. *R*
8. *B.* Remember "Journey to the Center of the Mind"?
9. *T*
10. *J.* This group performed the first version of "White Rabbit."
11. *A.* John Bonham came to Led Zeppelin from the same band.
12. S
13. *D.* The Poney's only hit, "Different Drum," was written by Monkee Mike Nesmith.
14. *K*
15. *I*
16. *G*
17. *C*
18. *H*
19. *Q*
20. *O*

ANSWERS

BETWEEN THE LINES

- **A.** "Subterranean Homesick Blues," Bob Dylan (this line inspired the radical group Weatherman, later the Weather Underground)
- **B.** "Stairway to Heaven," Led Zeppelin
- **C.** "Won't Get Fooled Again," The Who
- **D.** "Bennie and the Jets," Elton John
- **E.** "Lola," The Kinks
- **F.** "Sympathy for the Devil," the Rolling Stones
- **G.** "Year of the Cat," Al Stewart
- **H.** "A Day in the Life," The Beatles
- **I.** "The End," The Doors
- **J.** "Born to Run," Bruce Springsteen
- **K.** 'White Rabbit," Jefferson Airplane (extra points if you said The Great Society, Grace Slick's first group)
- **L.** "Purple Haze," Jimi Hendrix
- **M.** "Sir Duke," Stevie Wonder
- **N.** "I Get Around," The Beach Boys
- **O.** "The Boxer," Simon and Garfunkel
- **P.** "Roundabout," Yes
- **Q.** "Don't Stand So Close to Me," The Police
- **R.** "Tutti Frutti," Little Richard
- **S.** "Born to Be Wild," Steppenwolf (is this the first song to use the phrase "heavy metal"?)

THE IVY LEAGUE ROCK AND ROLL QUIZ BOOK

ANSWERS

WHO WROTE THE BOOK OF LOVE

1. D
2. E
3. C
4. F
5. G
6. A
7. H
8. B
9. J
10. I
11. Jim Morrison, by Jerry Hopkins and Danny Sugarman
12. Janis Joplin, by Myra Friedman
13. The Beatles—the best book about this much-dissected group, by Philip Norman
14. Phil Ochs, by Marc Eliot
15. Bruce Springsteen, by Dave Marsh
16. Jerry Lee Lewis, by Nick Tosches
17. Hank Williams, by Chet Flippo
18. Jimi Hendrix, by David Henderson
19. Frank Zappa and the Mothers of Invention, by David Walley
20. Keith Moon, by his aide Dougal Butler

ANSWERS

DIFFERENT DRUM

1. The Who. I sincerely hope you got this question right.
2. The Go-Gos
3. Earth, Wind, & Fire. White writes for and produces the group as well.
4. The Jefferson Airplane
5. The Beach Boys
6. The E Street Band
7. The Clash
8. The Doors
9. Led Zeppelin
10. Kiss. Criss was the guy with the cat makeup.
11. The indomitable Stewart Copeland
12. Mitch Mitchell
13. Charlie Watts, easily the Stones' most consistent musician.
14. Mick Avory
15. Levon Helm, a fine singer as well.
16. Doug Clifford, not nearly as fine a singer.
17. Micky Dolenz, whose singing we shall not address in this tasteful book.
18. Chris Frantz
19. Ringo Starr, who only took one drum solo in the entire Beatles *oeuvre*: "The End," on *Abbey Road*.
20. Bun E. Carlos, who looks more like an accountant.

ANSWERS

NO BASSIST IN FACT

1. The Who
2. The Pretenders
3. The Allman Brothers Band
4. The Talking Heads (extra credit for her solo project, the Tom Tom Club)
5. The Sex Pistols
6. Pink Floyd
7. Squeeze
8. The Police
9. Chicago
10. The Animals. Chandler later managed Jimi Hendrix.
11. John Paul Jones, who also played keyboards
12. Garry Tallent
13. Paul Simonon
14. Stu Cook
15. The stalwart Bill Wyman
16. Kathy Valentine
17. John McVie, whose name provides the group Fleetwood with their Mac
18. Chris Squire
19. Phil Lesh
20. Gene Simmons, the guy who spits blood and stuff like that

ROCK LOCKS

1. Jimi Hendrix
2. Elvis Presley (who else?)
3. Bob Marley
4. Grace Jones
5. Debra Harry
6. The Beatles
7. Rod Stewart
8. The very early Who
9. Cindy Wilson and Kate Pierson from the B-52's
10. Adam Ant

ANSWERS

JUKE BOX HEROES

1. The Who, natch
2. Heart
3. Grand Funk Railroad ("Barechested, and proud of it!")
4. Rush
5. The Grateful Dead (you were expecting maybe Van Halen?)
6. ZZ Top
7. Chic
8. The Rolling Stones
9. Jethro Tull
10. The Jam
11. Brian May
12. Andy Summers
13. Robbie Krieger (who wrote "Light My Fire" and a lot more of their best songs than you—or Jim Morrison—suspected)
14. The late James Honeyman-Scott
15. Rick Nielsen, Huntz Hall look-alike
16. Robbie Robertson (described by Bob Dylan as playing "mathematical guitar")
17. Frank Marino (who claims to be possessed by Jimi Hendrix)
18. Mark Knopfler
19. Dave Davies
20. Buck Dharma

ANSWERS

CRY OF LOVE

1. Van Morrison
2. Blue Oyster Cult
3. The Ramones
4. Funkadelic
5. The Rolling Stones
6. Sly and the Family Stone
7. The MC5
8. Devo
9. The Charlie Daniels Band
10. Muddy Waters

LOVE THAT DIRTY WATER

1. Rain
2. Water
3. River
4. Creek
5. Lake
6. Sea
7. Surf
8. Flood
9. Wave
10. Tears

ANSWERS

DANCING IN THE STREET

1. *G*
2. *E* (The Twist was invented by Hank Ballard of the Midnighters)
3. *I*
4. *D*
5. *B* (the flip side of "The Wanderer")
6. *H* (Brown once did a disc called "It's A New Day, So Let A Man Come In and Do The Popcorn")
7. *F*
8. *A* (Rufus Thomas, father of Stax songstress Carla Thomas, favored "Walking the Dog" when not occupied with his chicken)
9. *J*
10. *C* (Now It Can Be Told Department: Little Eva was the 16-year-old babysitter of Carole King's daughter, Louise Goffin)

EXTRA CREDIT: *Sid Vicious of the Sex Pistols*

THE IVY LEAGUE ROCK AND ROLL QUIZ BOOK
ANSWERS

SPEAKING WORDS OF WISDOM

1. Muddy Waters, who knows what he's talking about
2. Cat Stevens
3. David Byrne, Talking Head and guru of New York rock
4. Johnny Rotten (a.k.a. John Lydon)
5. Ted Nugent
6. The modest Sid Vicious
7. Frank Sinatra in 1957. In 1969, Ol' Blue Eyes added that George Harrison's "Something" was "the greatest love song of the last fifty years."
8. John Denver
9. Timothy Leary

HE'S SO FINE

1. Johnny
2. Mr. Jones
3. Joe DiMaggio
4. Sam
5. Major Tom
6. Jack
7. Lido, of course
8. Bill
9. Eddie
10. Mr. Jimmy

ANSWERS

FEEL LIKE A NUMBER

1. Keith
2. Tommy Tutone
3. Three Dog Night
4. Alice Cooper
5. Zager and Evans, who mercifully disappeared soon after
6. The Crests
7. The Mamas and the Papas
8. Chicago, who have a thing about numbers (look at their album titles)
9. Jimi Hendrix
10. Gary "U.S." Bonds, who got his nickname when his manager found a package of "Buy U.S. Bonds" stickers and stuck them on disc jockey copies of "Quarter to Three." The DJs thought it was a public service announcement and played the song

ANSWERS

GIRLS TALK

1. I
2. E
3. C
4. O
5. B
6. H
7. K
8. N
9. A
10. G
11. M
12. D
13. L
14. J
15. F

THE IVY LEAGUE ROCK QUIZ

1. C
2. F
3. B
4. D
5. A
6. E

EXTRA CREDIT: *Sha Na Na*

ANSWERS

MYSTERY ROCK STARS

1. Believe it or not, Ted Nugent began his youthful career specializing in liturgical music!
2. Yes, it's the one and only Elvis who's serious expression enhances his early cherubic appeal.
3. It's Ann Wilson, undoubtedly playing "You Gotta Have Heart" in this early family photograph.
4. Ozzy Osbourne has grown into the quintessential rock and roll gourmand. Never let it be said that audiences, or Ozzy himself for that matter, leave an Osbourne concert hungry!
5. By now, Rod Stewart must know that being sexy is something that comes naturally to a handsome British rocker like himself.
6. The music of Barry, Maurice and Robin Gibb, also known as the fabulous Bee Gees, has taken America by storm and has given a whole new meaning to Saturday Night!
7. Known as Noah Drake to "General Hospital" fans, his real name, Rick Springfield is known by many, many more.
8. Though she is not yet a Blondie, that pretty little girl in the picture is unmistakably Debra Harry.
9. Brian Jones at the age of three had no idea that he would grow up to found The Rolling Stones, a band that has outlived Brian himself, but that owes its success to his innate genius.

THE IVY LEAGUE ROCK AND ROLL QUIZ BOOK

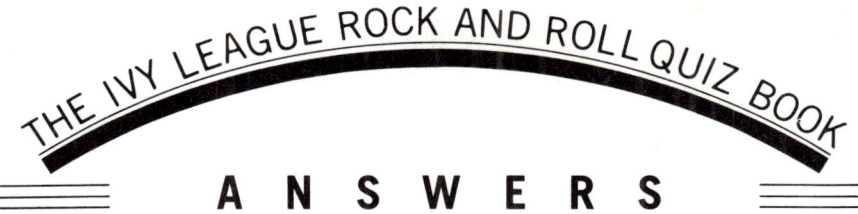

ANSWERS

10. Some things have become more private to REO Speedwagon's Kevin Cronin, but he makes no secret of the fact that he likes to "Keep the Fire Burning!"

11. The young Barry Manilow's expression seems to indicate a knowledge of the riches and fame that adulthood would bring. Such self-assuredness is indeed unusual for a tyke still in short pants!